TALKING
FASHION

TALKING
FASHION

FROM NICK KNIGHT TO RAF SIMONS
IN THEIR OWN WORDS

JAN KEDVES

PRESTEL

MUNICH · LONDON · NEW YORK

PREFACE

Fashion is, of course, much more than what designers create. To truly understand the phenomenon of fashion one has to look at related fields as well – and ask, for instance, how clothes are staged by photographers, how they are worn by models and stars, how journalists and bloggers write about collections, and how conglomerates market their brands. The work of curators who exhibit fashion and of theorists and historians who evaluate it from a scholarly standpoint also forms an important part of the picture. That is why in Talking Fashion experts from a number of different fields are given a voice – in 25 in-depth conversations. This book features, among many others, photographer Juergen Teller, whose pictures are famous for their irony (see the photo of Victoria Beckham on the cover), alongside the legendary model Veruschka, who often found fashion photography simply too boring when working in the industry in the 1960s; or dancer Willi Ninja, whose art of vogueing was heavily influenced by fashion images (and who had an appreciable influence on fashion in return), is portrayed next to a designer like Raf Simons, who often drew inspiration from underground cultures (such as vogueing) for his collections.

These conversations present a variety of personal experiences, critical reflections and anecdotes. I conducted them between late 2005 and June 2013. Many of them have appeared – in shorter or longer form – in Spex, the German pop culture magazine for which I worked as an editor from 2007 to 2010 and served as editor-in-chief from autumn 2010 until spring 2012. Other conversa-

tions were commissioned by Zoo, *a fashion magazine published in Amsterdam, by the German daily newspaper* Die Welt *and by* Groove, *a magazine devoted to electronic club music. Two conversations – the ones with Helmut Lang and fashion theorist Barbara Vinken – were conducted in collaboration with the Berlin literary scholar and art historian Philipp Ekardt. I spoke with three people specifically for this book – illustrator Jean-Paul Goude, designer Iris van Herpen and photographer Viviane Sassen.*

Do these conversations present a consistent picture of fashion? That was certainly not the goal. An interest in the people themselves, their work and their individual views of fashion always took precedence. Yet there are certain recurring themes. One is the digitization of our lives and its – usually positive but occasionally problematic – impact on fashion: from blogging, Photoshop and 3D printing to the global levelling of local styles of dress. The subject of the changing role of the body in fashion also comes up several times: are clothes today, in an era of omnipresent body styling, still worn for the purpose of giving posture, or a habitus to the body, or is it up to the hard-worked body to provide posture on its own – while clothes merely put the effects of that work on display? A number of my interview partners also talked about economic issues: how can an independent brand survive in the new millennium? Should one go along with the ever-shorter cycles in which collections are dumped on the market, or is there a more sustainable way of creating fashion? And last but not least, should one want to seek refuge under the roof of a conglomerate like LVMH or PPR (now Kering)?

In the preface to a book like this, which brings together a number of different perspectives yet always maintains faith in the spoken word, I should probably point out that of course the relationship between journalism and the fashion industry is not all sweetness and light. The conditions for arranging an interview with a curator like Valerie Steele or a documentary film-maker like Loïc Prigent are relatively uncomplicated. But anyone who wishes to speak with a designer has a number of hurdles to negotiate. The PR department of the brand in question has to take a favourable view of the interviewer, and the medium for which the interview is requested must be regarded as sufficiently important. But above all there has to be a fitting occasion, for if a designer or brand is not in the process of launching a new line or opening a new shop or exhibition, most PR agents will see no reason to seek publicity in the form of an in-depth interview. Anyone who is lucky enough to land an appointment would do well to avoid asking overly critical questions – unless he wants to be erased from the contact list. Perhaps that is why interviews in the field of fashion often tend to read like mere press briefings in disguise. The goal of a journalistic interview, however, must of course always be to bring out more than a rehearsed PR text.

Thus interviews like these are truly rewarding – conversations with the objective of realizing a different and more profound way of talking fashion; conversations that reveal the diversity and complexity of fashion. I sincerely hope that readers will enjoy reading and looking through this book.

Jan Kedves

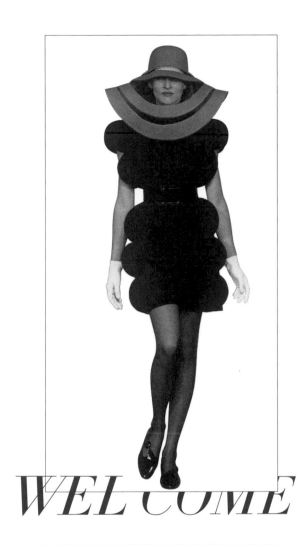

WELCOME

Jean-Paul GOUDE

FASHION ILLUSTRATOR

Paris

Jean-Paul Goude is one of the greatest iconographers of the last half-century, working like virtually no other at the crossroads of fashion, advertising and art. The men and women in Goude's photos seem bigger, stronger, always more beautiful and sometimes a bit wilder than they really are. Goude, who was born in the Paris suburb of Saint-Mandé in 1940, perfected his own unique method of processing photographs as illustrations – which goes far beyond the limits of retouching – while serving as art director for *Esquire* in the 1970s. From his poster campaigns for the Galeries Lafayette, to his TV commercials for Chanel, to the countless portraits of his muse Grace Jones (with whom he has a son), practically all of Goude's oeuvre is unforgettable. Most recently, he contributed to the Kenzo hysteria with his X campaigns.

Monsieur Goude, are your glasses broken? They look like you fixed them with white duct tape.

My glasses are not broken and believe it or not, this little piece of white tape is nothing but another manifestation of my frantic obsession with style … just kidding! Yet the fact is that my eyes are set too close to each other. The tape on the glasses is just a graphic trick, an optical illusion, a white spot that structures one's features and that – according to me – corrects the problem.

You seem to love such optical illusions. For example in your book *So Far So Goude*, published in 2005, you explain how – as a teenager – you came up with ways to make your shoulders appear a little broader and your legs longer.

As far as I can remember, I've always been very preoccupied with my appearance. When I was a little kid, I wondered why I didn't look as good as the other guys. For example, why didn't I look good in blue jeans? I had no idea at the time that my legs were too short compared with my upper body and that my head was too big for my shoulders. I started noticing these things around adolescence. By the time I reached 16 or 17, I was already doctoring my own clothes.

In your book you call it 'prosthesis'.

Well, in a way, some clothes are nothing but prostheses, which are very often taken for granted. A shoulder pad in a jacket, for instance, nobody notices, whereas a shoulder pad in a T-shirt is considered ridiculous, when actually both devices accomplish the same mission: to improve one's silhouette. I won't mention high-heeled shoes or platforms, which are obvious prostheses that everyone accepts. The same thing is true about wearing a jacket, the waist of which is cut higher than it is *au naturel*; it gives the illusion of longer legs, etc.… Of course, these graphic tricks should be as subtle as possible – one doesn't want to look like a living caricature. After all, the goal is to seduce, to be more sexually attractive.

In the late 1960s, you put several insoles in normal-looking high-top trainers as part of your series *French Correction*, making the wearer six centimetres taller. The concept seems to have been

Basketball shoes from the *French Correction* series, 1970

adopted by Isabel Marant lately – she's making tons of money with her so-called 'wedge sneakers'.

Good for her. The *French Correction* was never meant to be commercialized anyway.

In *So Far So Goude*, there's a picture of your meeting with President François Mitterrand in 1988. At the time, you were commissioned by the French state to stage the bicentennial anniversary in July 1989 of the French Revolution. In the picture, you're wearing a red, hooded sweatshirt and an olive-coloured army jacket. Was that your way of dressing up for the occasion?

No, it was pure coincidence. The meeting with President Mitterrand was very early in the morning, and we had just flown in from China, where we had been casting amateur dancers and musicians for the bicentennial parade. We were taken directly from the airport to the Élysée Palace to report to the President. We didn't have a chance to change clothes. I think Mitterrand actually welcomed this type of informality.

You wore your white-taped glasses in a recent TV documentary, too, in which you talked about the legendary Italian fashion illustrator René Gruau. In what way was he important to you?

Gruau was my childhood idol. When I was a kid, he was a huge star, his posters were all over Paris. So, when I decided to become an artist, Gruau was definitively on my mind. Another hero of mine, who unfortunately never became as successful as Gruau, was Tom Keogh, whose erotic drawings I adored. All this explains why my early drawings were so influenced both by Gruau and Keogh. I forgot to tell you, I was about 20 years old when I met this aggressive young agent who couldn't make up his mind whether or not I was worthy enough to join his stable of illustrators. When he mentioned that he represented Gruau, I told him: 'If you really want to know whether I'm good enough for you, why don't you take my drawings and show them to him. He'll tell you!' And that's exactly what Gruau did!

Wow, you must have been very flattered.

Yes, I was on cloud nine. Especially when Gruau called my mother to tell her that I should continue drawing.

So this was all in the 1950s?

Yes, the very late 50s.

Wasn't that when the big era of fashion illustration was actually over already because of the increasing demand for fashion photography?

Indeed it was. My admiration for Gruau made me choose a dying profession; I don't hold grudges. I still worship him.

You reversed the development later in your own work: you took up photography, but only in order to produce raw material for your illustrations. You cut up photographs, retouched them and painted on them.

This is why I can't call myself a photographer per se; I'm more like a graphic artist who manipulates photography, which is different. My career as a traditional fashion illustrator was only very short. Obsessed by making as much money as possible and as quickly as I could, I was turning out mediocre advertising campaigns like hot cakes in the 60s. That's to say my production was getting worse and worse as time went

Azzedine and Farida, 1984

Constructivist maternity dress for Grace Jones, 1979

by. After three years, my career as a fashion illustrator was over. I was 24. So I started working in different areas, using any kind of technique I could handle – photography, film, stage design, and so on. Only to finally realize that technique isn't everything. It's one's point of view that counts. The way one sees the world. No matter how it's expressed.

What's your take on Photoshop, then? There's no difference between photography and illustration in Photoshop. A few clicks enable you to do what, back then, you did tediously by hand, only much faster.

True, and I use it all the time. But Photoshop is just a machine, a wonderful machine, depending on who works it. If you don't have a point of view, you can play around with Photoshop as long as you want, you'll never find it.

It'd be interesting to talk about another fashion illustrator with whom you were friends and who has been rediscovered lately: Antonio Lopez.

Antonio was a gem, an exceptional fashion artist, a supreme draughtsman, as well as a very charismatic person. He and Juan Ramos – his very own art director and partner – were a creative team, while Corey Tippin advised on make-up. In 1979, I produced an eight-page story for *Esquire* entitled 'Antonio's girls'. Antonio and I lived across the street from each other at Union Square, and we'd hang out together every so often. His studio was like a mini Factory, very stimulating.

Antonio was supposedly responsible for discovering Grace Jones while she was still a model, before she started singing. Is that true?

I don't think so. Antonio probably photographed Grace when she was signed to a modelling agency and was laboriously commuting from Paris to New York, but then so were Peter Knapp, Hans Feurer, Francis Giacobetti and Oliviero Toscani … I'd say Yves Saint Laurent himself was the one who gave Grace that push both as a model and as a budding entertainer. Disco did the rest, and my contribution came later. Antonio loved Grace. But at the time we collaborated with each other, his favourite models were Pat Cleveland, Donna Jordan, Eija, Patti d'Arbanville, and especially Jerry Hall, his favourite muse and great love. Which brings us to the only time I ever collaborated with Antonio and Juan on a project of my own.

You mean Grace Jones' Constructivist dress?

Exactly. It was 1979 and Grace was eight months pregnant by me. She wanted the child but she also wanted and needed to promote her new album, in spite of her condition. Something had to be done. This is when I came up with this mega-maternity Cubist dress idea that would hopefully solve the problem. I called Antonio and Juan for help. At the time, anything that had to do with Cubism or Constructivism was very much in the air. Klaus Nomi was the man of the hour, and Antonio, Juan and myself were Bauhaus crazy. So, I brought along my books on Constructivism to their studio, and we went to work.

You took many images of Grace Jones in the late 1970s and early 1980s that are iconic to this day. So when you reunited with her in 2009 to shoot a portrait for *V Magazine*, there was the danger of producing something weaker. But the result – which also celebrated the 30th anniversary of your private and working relationship – turned out iconic again. Were you surprised yourself?

Grace Jones for *V Magazine*, 2009

> *'I became determined to do everything I could to turn things around to Grace's advantage.'*

Indeed I was, very agreeably so, though this time I was only involved as the photographer. All I had to do for the cover of *V Magazine* was record Grace as she posed in her hat created by Philip Treacy.

No fighting, no arguing?

Absolutely none. If Grace and I fought a lot, a long time ago, I never forced her – or anybody else for that matter – to do anything. I couldn't have, and didn't even try. I suggested, demonstrated, lured, enticed, persuaded, even rescued her more than anything.

Rescued her in what way?

Let's say, by 'protecting her reputation'. I like 'rescue', it's more dramatic, but it's too much. When Grace was pregnant, I came to Paris to visit my mother while Grace stayed at home with soon-to-be-born Paulo. Here I was at Kenzo's, standing in front of the cashier, paying for a small gift for the future mother, when I overheard two young women – pretty hip-looking – putting down Grace in the most malicious manner. They were claiming that Grace's career had hit rock-bottom in Paris, and how nobody cared about her anymore, and that she was finished once and for all … That was my girlfriend they were talking about! I was so shocked, I couldn't react. But more importantly, I realized what a dangerous position Grace was in at the time – professionally speaking, of course. I took this incident as an omen. And from that moment on, I became determined to do everything I could to turn things around to her advantage.

You just mentioned Kenzo. In 2012 and 2013, you did campaigns for their new creative team, Carol Lim and Humberto Leon.

The X campaigns, yes!

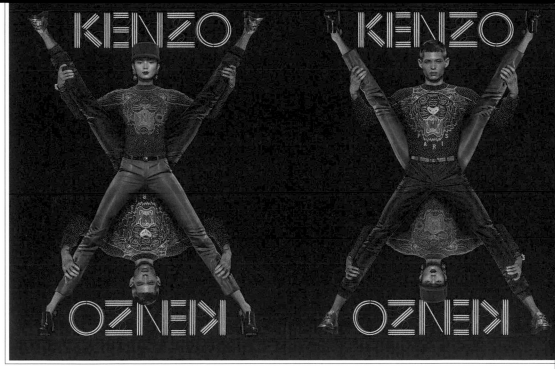

The first X campaign for Kenzo, autumn/winter 2012/13

How did that come about?
Well, Carol and Humberto contacted me and said they'd been hired by LVMH to take over Kenzo, and that they had me in mind for their next advertising campaign. We met for lunch, and I found them very charming. They're both American. Humberto is part Chinese, and Carol's family comes from Korea. Since my wife is also an Asian-American, we had a lot to talk about: Japan, Korea, China, potential problems, hip-hop, kung fu, mangas … very interesting!
Did you talk about jungles, too? The whole Kenzo aesthetic is very much centred around jungles.
Indeed we did. In fact, we had barely been seated more than ten minutes when they mentioned *Jungle Fever*, my old book from 1981, and how perfectly – I quote – my 'aesthetics' would fit with the brand's spirit. I loved that straight-to-the-point attitude.
Could you explain the iconic X symbol you came up with?
At first I thought about recycling a picture I had done years before, but it didn't feel right. I shot it anyway, but the idea for the X started to take shape in my mind when the Kenzo neon sign was brought into the studio, suddenly giving it a 'showbizzy' atmosphere. And since I had showbiz on my mind, why not choreograph our two models, like dancers on the stage of a theatre, and craft an image that would allow the viewer to look either at the boy or at the girl by simply shifting the printed ad around? You know, like one does with playing cards.
When looking at the ads, one doesn't realize it immediately – but of course you've altered the limbs of the models and made them a bit longer.

Mounia in Saint Laurent, 1985

I had to, because with normal proportions you'd have a hard time holding that pose with the same effortless elegance as the two kids did. Actually, I saw 12-year-old Kenzo fans practising the X during recess, in junior high school, on the internet!

That makes you responsible for some sexy new couples?

I hope so!

You said that you thought about recycling an idea for Kenzo. You seem to do that quite often. For example, there was a predecessor for the legendary cover image for Grace Jones' Slave to the Rhythm album – the cut-up mouth – namely the image of model Mounia wearing Saint Laurent from 1985. And your spot for Chanel's Égoïste perfume in 1990 was based on an earlier idea that you couldn't carry out.

Let me tell you about the *Égoïste* saga: it all started with a project I had with Farida …

Farida Khelfa?

Yes. Farida was the woman who followed Grace in my life. She had written an extraordinary poem based on an incident she had witnessed during her childhood in the projects in the suburbs of Lyons, where she lived with her family and hundreds of other immigrants, mostly of North African descent. My goal was to take her poem as the basis for a mini pop opera for French television. What fascinated me when I went down to Lyons to do some location scouting was this gigantic drab forest of grey, high-rise buildings riddled with hundreds of windows; and behind every window, I imagined a woman, in a *hijab*, staring outside, sort of spying. As soon as one of the women witnessed something going wrong in the street, they'd all lean out of the windows and scream out their disapproval, before brutally slamming the shutters: *boom, bam, bam, boom*, very strong! Needless to say, the project never got off the ground; a bit too radical I guess and much too expensive for French TV. Coincidentally, six months later, I got a call from Chanel, whose creative director asked me if I had an idea for *Égoïste*, the new scent for men that they were getting ready to launch. I said: 'Well, I might have something …'

So the projects in the banlieue became a luxurious palace, and the Arab women …

… were turned into models wearing Chanel gowns, screaming their lungs out to the wind. A good idea is a good idea. It would have been a pity not to use it in one way or another.

And so one could really say that you've always approached your commercial commissions as an artist?

Égoïste film set, Rio de Janeiro, 1990

I think I have, since from the very beginning I chose to take advertising and style as pre-requisites for an artistic career. For example, my *Goudemalion* exhibition at the Musée des Arts Décoratifs in 2011 was an artistic project. The show in itself was the work of art and it made total sense. It told the trials and tribulations of this character called Goudemalion, from his early childhood to this day: Saint-Mandé, cowboys, Indians, African warriors, tigers, the *French Correction*, Toukie, Grace, Farida, HRH the Queen of Seoul – everything and everybody was there. The show was a big success. I'm lucky!

Is it true that a few years ago, when you found out that a new house was going to be built right in front of your house in Belleville, where you live, you went and bought the airspace in the top floors of the future building to prevent it from blocking your view?

Yes I did, but let me try to explain. Years ago, I bought a little house built on the flank of a very steep hill in the Buttes Chaumont, a charming neighbourhood in the north of Paris, where we lived, my wife, my kids and I. The panoramic view of Paris from our garden was breathtaking. One day, I saw a big crane stick out at the end of the garden and realized that someone was preparing the construction of a building that would not only block our view completely, but considerably shrink the value of my little house. So, I made a deal directly with the promoter: I would buy the air of the two future floors of his building, and when its construction reached the level of my garden, I would turn those two floors into one big studio for myself. Nowadays, I just have to cross my garden to go to work. And I still have my view of Sacré Coeur and the Eiffel Tower. I added more trees and bushes in the garden: it's a jungle out there, really!

Rick OWENS

FASHION DESIGNER
Paris

Rick Owens is a prime example of a designer from the underground who has tenaciously maintained his independence despite growing success. Owens founded his label in 1994, and for many years his collections were sold exclusively by Charles Gallay in Los Angeles. Born in Porterville, California, in 1961, Owens achieved his breakthrough with the CFDA Emerging Talent Award in 2002 and soon moved on to Paris, where he lives today. His aesthetic – hedonistic, sombre and always a bit ghostly – is often referred to as 'haute goth'. Owens, who in 2005 began designing furniture, too, is married to his muse, Michèle Lamy, an important patron of designer Gareth Pugh. His company, Rick Owens Corp, is located in the regal Place du Palais-Bourbon directly opposite Condé Nast.

I'd say that this might be one of the reasons for my success. A lot of my clients appreciate the fact that Rick Owens does not advertise, and I assume that if I started doing ads I would alienate a lot of these clients – they would somehow start suspecting my purity. The manipulation of fashion through advertising has become so transparent nowadays, people are aware of every single marketing device that's being used to seduce them. I don't think this is going to work for very much longer. So I guess I am lucky that my label could go without advertising right from the start.

Do you have an explanation for this?

Well, the clothes I designed did sell right away. I took them myself to the stores in Los Angeles where I wanted them to be sold. Granted, I was lucky to meet retailers who were pioneers in fashion; they took a lot of risks on new designers. When they added my collection to their range it sold well immediately. So I gained a reputation for providing clothes that the stores could sell, and I think that established me more than by being featured in magazines or creating hype. I'm not criticizing people who do it another way. But I came more from a retail side, not so much from an editorial side.

Another interesting fact about your business is that you do not sell perfume – normally it's fragrances that generate the largest revenue for fashion labels.

Well, actually I'm in the process of creating a perfume – I'm working on one with a perfumer in Paris, and I'm wearing it myself. But to be honest, I don't know how to sell it. You know, the perfume business works totally differently from the clothing business. Not doing advertising for a perfume would be commercial suicide because there's no way to start a perfume on a small scale. Developing a fragrance and getting it ready for the market is very expensive. So if I launched a fragrance on my own, I would be lucky to break even, and in the context of designer fragrances, mine would probably still look like a weakling. I'd like a little more for my labour of love than that. On the other hand, if I cooperated with a big company, as other designers do, the company would invest strongly in the perfume, and they would expect me to do a big advertising campaign. What would that do to the rest of my company? It would change everything. All of a sudden I'd become a designer who advertises. So the whole thing probably would smell of selling out.

'When it comes to self-referentiality and the use of codes that are almost subliminal, I sometimes think fashion operates on an equal level with contemporary art.'

Look from Rick Owens' Lilies line, spring/summer 2013

Interestingly, it's especially rappers who have recently done free advertising for you: Jay-Z raps about your leather jackets in his track 'Ultra', as does Rick Ross in his hit single 'Super High'.

I must admit that I'm not that familiar with their music, or with hip-hop in general. I mainly listen to hardcore techno, old disco records and old show tunes. But of course I'm pleased to have a happy client, and I think it is nice that they talk about my products. I cannot imagine rejecting any positive response. I don't supply them with my jackets, if that's what you think. They have to go out and buy them. It is a surprise to me that they would even bother, but I guess as our world is getting more and more commercial maybe it has become interesting to them to look into less obvious, more obscure fashion labels. Before, hip-hop used to be all about big luxury brands like, you know, Louis Vuitton, Chanel and Gucci.

You are regarded as the modern master of the bias cut. What makes this technique so important for your work?

Regarding bias cut, I like the technical simplicity of using the cling of the fabric to fit the body. Using bias, you cut diagonally to the grain of a fabric. This way you get natural, flowing shapes instead of overconstructing a silhouette or stretching the fabric too much. Madeleine Vionnet, the Parisian designer, was the master of the bias cut in the early 20th century. Her dresses influenced the aesthetic of black-and-white Hollywood movies and its divas.

Madeleine Vionnet's dresses were supposedly inspired by antique marble statues, and she aimed for the apparent weightlessness of the folds in the dresses of Greek goddesses.

Greek goddesses are not so important for my aesthetic. But Catholicism is in there – or to be more precise: the idea of monks and nuns in long black gowns trailing through dusty temples. I was brought up very Catholic. It probably comes from there.

A few years ago you started designing furniture besides doing clothing. Your pieces have been shown in galleries and exhibitions. Do you regard your furniture as art?

I guess you could say that they are a kind of functional art, but I do not think about that question too much. Art, fashion, design … I do not really see the need to differentiate.

Why not?

You know, I started out wanting to be a painter. I went to Parsons School of Design in Los Angeles for two years in the 1980s, studying art there. But then I got intimidated because I thought I would never be able to intellectually have the energy to keep up with art. I probably was too impressed by the 'Gesamtkunstwerk' of artists I admired: Brancusi, Beuys, Bacon … I loved them not only for their kind of rough, heroic flamboyance, but part of the satisfaction in their art for me was seeing a full story, an artist's life work. So I went into fashion because I thought that it was a lot more superficial.

But it's not?

Not at all! I sometimes even suspect that fashion has kind of surpassed art intellectually. You know, when it comes to self-referentiality and the use of codes that are almost subliminal, I sometimes think that fashion operates on an equal level with art – at least with contemporary art. But fashion seems to still have something a little bit more supernatural and mysterious happening there, while art often tends to be about ironic comments and teaching us a lesson. You know, all these artists making jokey works about the fact that their art is expensive and so on …

Your furniture designs almost look like mysterious sculptures – one might even call them monoliths.

Yes, I wanted my furniture to look immovable. A marble armchair as I have designed it is not supposed to be practical. It's not supposed to be moved, it stays there with you forever – until you die or until the house burns down. I guess I see my furniture as a bit of a reaction to the idea of inexpensive design that is so prevalent today. We have got Ikea, so it's not my job to design things for people living in small, single apartments who move to the next single apartment every few months.

Do you design the furniture for yourself?

That's how I started. I basically did the furniture because I moved into this big house that I bought a few years ago on Place du Palais-Bourbon in Paris. This is the house that used to be the headquarters for the French Socialist Party. I live there with Michèle, my wife, and I also run my business from there. When we moved in, the house had been unoccupied for a few years.

So did you find things that President François Mitterrand had left behind when he moved out?

No, but the old office cubicles were still in there, so we had to tear them out. My idea was to have the house entirely furnished in Jean-Michel Frank and Robert Mallet-Stevens, but I couldn't afford to fill the house with their pieces. Old Art Deco furniture is so expensive! Besides, all the Art Deco furniture is so small, especially for an American. You know, Americans are famous for overdoing everything, we make everything bigger. Plus we like fakes. So I decided to just build the furniture myself.

Stag antler stool from Rick Owens' furniture collection

I took Art Deco and Bauhaus ideas in portions and exaggerated them, I simplified them, made them more monolithic and dark.

<u>But don't Art Deco und Bauhaus derive from two totally opposite concepts of design?</u>

Conceptually, maybe. But if you look at them more closely, I feel there is a similarity in their spareness and their idea of grace. Both styles aim for a rational, graceful line from point A to point B – at least the more simple, demure Art Deco style that I had in mind. So I guess you could say I started doing furniture in the same way that I started designing clothes in the early 1990s: at first I had no clue, I had not gone to school for it or anything, so I faked it. Which is exactly what I did when I first started making clothes.

<u>You are probably the only contemporary designer who uses deer antlers and human skulls in his furniture.</u>

Believe it or not, I got these skulls on the internet. There is a company on the net that provides human skulls for medical research. I use them for my furniture. Each of them has documentation – so it's not like I found these skulls on the back seat of a car or something. You really can get all you want on the internet these days!

<u>And the antlers?</u>

I always loved antlers, I refer to them as brutalist crowns. I love the heroism they exude. To me they are a symbol of glory.

<u>If you sat down on one of your antler benches the wrong way it would probably also look very heroic – you might get skewered.</u>

Which would be such a beautiful way to die, don't you think?

<u>Where does your fascination with death come from? Your clothes often also look quite morbid – your favourite colour seems to be the black of the Goths.</u>

Well, everybody is fascinated with death, I am certainly not the only one. I just like the idea of acknowledging it. All of those magazine covers that are talking about young starlets that might have a drug problem, all of that is about sex and death, and we love it! Anybody will stop on the street to look at an accident, especially if there is somebody young and beautiful dying – that makes it all the more exciting for us. Sex and death, these are the things that get us going, that's just human nature.

<u>But it seems that you yourself want to play a trick on death – judging from the determination with which you have excercised and toughened your body over the years.</u>

I do not work out for health reasons, I do it purely for vanity. People refer to working out as just another addiction, and it is. I don't care. You see, I was growing up in this very conservative, very stiff little town. I come from Porterville, California. In Catholic school I had to pray the Rosary and learn everything about the saints. I was a young little sissy and it was terrible for me – even though all these stories of heroic people in their elegant long robes held a certain aesthetic appeal for me. But as soon as I got out, my life became the total opposite. I had a very indulgent, extreme time in the 1980s and really went as far as I could. I guess I attacked losing control with the same discipline that I had suffered from in my childhood. Today the cycle has turned again: I attack pumping my muscles with as much passion as I attacked going out three days on speed, like I used to.

<u>You once said that working out is like modern couture.</u>

Yes, I do believe that working out is like couture because it takes as much time and commitment. In the old days of couture you would spend hours and hours in the atelier, doing fittings, with all the handiwork involved. Now you spend hours and hours at the gym. It's kind of another version of the same thing.

It seems that especially fashion designers tend to obsess about the shaping of their bodies. Karl Lagerfeld, John Galliano, Thierry Mugler ...

I think that's because as a fashion designer you can become disillusioned with clothes and the magic that they can do after a while. You want more, something more extreme. And as a designer, where can you go except to sculpt your actual human flesh? I did not naturally turn out the way I imagined myself, so I had to manipulate what I had the

Look from Rick Owens' DRKSHDW line,
spring/summer 2011

only way I could. Believe me, I would have loved to be one of those languid white youths from a Gustave Moreau painting, but I had an Aztec nose and puffy nipples. By working out I was aiming for a mix of Joe Dallesandro and Iggy Pop. This is what I came up with – not too close, but not too far. To be honest, I think steroids are fantastic.

Speaking of vanity: in an exhibition of your furniture designs in New York you showed a bedroom with a big white alabaster bed and long mink curtains. Those pieces could come right out of Joris-Karl Huysman's novel *À rebours*. They strongly recall the era of decadence and dandyism.

Of course! I sell *À rebours* in all of my stores, in Paris, London, New York and Tokyo. I also sell the biography of Robert de Montesquiou, who was one of the first dandies. I'm a big fan of these books. When I was little, they were the only books in my parents' library that promised a bit of extravagance. I have to say that I was very lucky with my parents because even though they were very conservative we had a fantastic library. There was not only the Bible but also Huysmans, de Montesquiou and Oscar Wilde. I naturally gravitated towards these books. So the decadence and the symbolist period of the *fin de siècle* were very important to me in my formative years. For example, I love how in *À rebours* the protagonist Jean des Esseintes has his house full of Gustave Moreau paintings. I love Moreau's paintings and I love how in the Gustave Moreau museum in Paris there are many pictures of Salomé. Salomé is of course also a libretto written by Oscar Wilde, and Richard Strauss based his famous opera *Salomé* on this. And there is also the connection with Robert de Montesquiou having supposedly been the inspiration for the character Jean des Esseintes in *À rebours* ... I just love all of those little connections and references.

That said, one might wonder why you use skulls and antlers in your furniture – but not tortoise shells …

You're thinking of Robert de Montesquiou's golden tortoise, which he supposedly kept in his house? Yes, in *À rebours* Huysmans describes this tortoise as being encrusted with diamonds all over, but the shell becomes too heavy, so the animal dies. To be honest, I had actually thought of doing something with tortoise shell with stones in it as a kind of reference to that, but tortoise shell is very hard to come by. You know, tortoises are an endangered species. I mean you can buy tortoise shell if you really want to, but it is not that easy. Buying human skulls on the internet is a lot easier!

The supreme rule of the dandy is to always make sure that his clothes are cut from the most exquisite fabrics, but they should never look new. Your label is known for using washed leather for biker jackets so they look worn and soft even when they are new.

You know, in fashion you never spare a trouble to make something look casual and effortless – even when in fact a lot of work and consideration go into it. A real dandy hands his new leather shoes to his butler for a year before he himself puts them on. We wash the leathers we use for our biker jackets in order to take away some of the stiffness and shine.

Why do you use leather so frequently in your collections?

I always say that my aesthetic is that of an Art Deco Gay Leather Bar. I love leather for all the references in it – fetishism, punk rock, aggression. Everybody has a moment when they want to feel tough, glamorous and slightly wicked. Leather is the perfect material for such moments. I also love the idea of corrupting a standard like the American leather biker jacket and watch it actually being worn on the streets. That is much more exciting to me than doing ball gowns that are awesome to look at but only wearable once and then they disappear into the closet. All the people who wear my leather jackets do this out of an urge to reject the mainstream and be identified as a unique individual – ending up as members of an identical-looking Rick Owens tribe. I love the sweet absurdity of that.

Would it be wrong to also describe your aesthetic as a counter-reaction to the traditional notion of American fashion and the colour palette of Californian sportswear?

Well, it is possible that my aesthetic shows a childish passive aggression or a puerile sense of rebellion against the look that I grew up with. But you know what they say: California sunshine casts a lot of shadows.

Look from Rick Owens' DRKSHDW line, spring/summer 2013

Nick KNIGHT

FASHION PHOTOGRAPHER
Richmond, London

One might call it a clear, almost compulsive embrace of the future: Nick Knight has welcomed practically each new technological advance, from Photoshop to 3D scanning to HD-quality digital cameras. Nor does the fashion photographer – who was born in London in 1958, was once a skinhead and produced legendary Yamamoto and Jil Sander campaigns in the 1980s and 1990s – regard the internet as a threat to his work. On the contrary, in 2000, he founded the trendsetting on-line fashion platform SHOWstudio.com. In the early years, the platform featured primarily fashion films, but has since been expanded to include interviews and live-streamed panel discussions of fashion shows. This interview with Knight was conducted in 2010.

Mr. Knight, why did you become a photographer?

I probably couldn't pin it down to one single reason, but part of it certainly was that I'm interested in seeing something I have not seen. There is a popular misconception about photography: that photographers show people what they see. It's quite the opposite. When you are taking a photograph you never really see the photograph you are taking. There is the moment when the flash goes off and the moment when the shutter goes down, and around these moments there are things happening that you do not see. You see them later in the photograph. So in a way as a photographer you are pre-empting something.

A glimpse into the future?

In a way, yes. When I'm taking a photograph there is always a certain amount of guessing what is going to happen. So I increasingly tend to think that photographers don't really work with their eyes so much – we work with some other sense, you know, intuition, or premonition. And that is what I find fascinating about fashion: it is a medium entirely based on the future. Fashion is talked about mostly in the future tense, it keeps one and a half years ahead of the rest of the world – it is always about the next collection, next collection! So to a certain degree the future is where I work as a fashion photographer – and I like that a lot.

In your work as a photographer you have always embraced technological and aesthetic innovation.

Right. Purism, realism, analogue fetishism – I never really got that whole approach, you know? Even when I just started photographing in 1979 at the College of Art and Design in Bournemouth and Poole I felt that photography was already on its deathbed. That is a hard thing to say maybe, but at that point photography was already starting to change. Home video was becoming popular, the first digital graphics tools were in development. As soon as I got into photography I wanted to change it. My fellow students were still aiming to live up to the old masters, Alfred Stieglitz or Edward Steichen; they would use Kodachrome to obtain 'realistic skin tones'. I was not interested in that. I started to look at Kurt Schwitters, at the photomontages from the Bauhaus or the Russian Constructivists; I was interested in people who would cut their pictures. I was painting on my negatives. So in a way I tried out everything that was not considered classical photography.

In the 1980s, you experimented with cross-processing, developing negative colour print film in the 'wrong' chemicals, which results in unusually strong colours and contrasts.

Right. I guess I wanted to take photography apart and push its parameters as far as I could. Which was probably due to the fact that I came from science to the arts. I had begun a degree in biology, thinking I would work in the medical field. But then I invested myself in photography, not knowing whether I would be any good at this or complete rubbish. So I tried to apply scientific parameters to artistic work – which might seem absurd, but it produced wonderful effects!

Is it true that sometime during the 1980s Juergen Teller was your assistant – for a single day?

That is true. Juergen came to see me. He said he had just moved to London and that he was a big fan of my work. So I looked through his portfolio and told him: 'Juergen, why do you want to waste your time? You have a very clear vision in your head, you already have *the thing*. I don't see what you could possibly learn here.' But he insisted. So we agreed that he would assist me for one day – so he would see that I could not teach him anything. And that's how it was.

At the moment of our conversation there is a new issue of *Vogue* at British news-stands with two big editorials by you, and you also photographed the cover with Lily Donaldson. In a previous interview you said: 'Magazines are not worth being printed anymore.' Isn't there a contradiction?

Well, I think the quote you are referring to goes along the lines of me saying the

Still from a film by Nick Knight with model Ming Xi for Hong Kong fashion retailer Lane Crawford (2013)

Still from Nick Knight's fashion film *Men in Tights* for Bernhard Willhelm's autumn/winter 2008/09 collection

communication medium that is the most exciting at the moment is probably the internet. Not the printed fashion magazine. I'm not saying that print is bad or wrong or not powerful, and I still love to work with print magazines. But they hold less of a thrill for me today, because I think moving images – film and video on the internet – are actually the better medium for showing fashion. Besides that, magazines have a fundamental timing problem. After the Paris shows or the Milan shows it usually takes 5 to 6 months until you start seeing the representation of the shows in print. Online you can see it on the same day. So in a way photoshoots in magazines no longer have a purpose other than to show: this is how Mario Testino sees it, and this is how it looks when Steven Klein shoots it. Which is nice – but people know the clothes already.

Is that why in 2000 you decided to launch the online fashion platform SHOWstudio.com?

Exactly. You can publish a fashion picture globally today with the press of a button, without going through anybody at Condé Nast or anybody else. I can upload a film just as quickly, in one second. The internet is instant. So I think it is a real revolution and it has happened in the last 15 years. With SHOWstudio our agenda is to push fashion forward into the future.

Prada, Yves Saint Laurent, Dior: most high fashion brands have started to produce videos that go along with their newest collections. Is the fashion industry slowly starting to grasp the potential of the fashion film?

They have no choice, if you ask me. When we first started SHOWstudio in 2000 the fashion industry was still very reactionary. Technically it still seemed stuck in the Stone Age. A lot of fashion editors did not have email, and a lot of designers, including some of the very good, would say: 'Oh no, I don't like computers, I'm not techy.' It has taken ten years and the beginning of a huge financial crisis to make people change. Now it is about the money, of course! I do not like financial crises because they will make a lot of misery for people, but the good thing about them is that they bring people to reevaluate systems. The fashion industry now looks at older formats like the fashion shows and magazine advertising in order to reevaluate them financially – which is not bad because it means they can actually try and understand different possibilities. You know, now they ask what are the 300 journalists who come to a fashion show, and what are 200 000 magazine buyers who flip through ads quickly, compared to the millions of people whom they can reach on the internet? The fashion film will profit from that, I'm sure.

What exactly is the fashion film?

First of all it is not some kind of music video for the fashion industry. In music videos the narrative follows the sound, in fashion film it is the other way around. Of course there is a soundtrack – sound and image are a very important coupling – but in fashion film the visual mustn't serve the music. The narrative is imbued in the pieces of clothing. When designers create clothes they have already put their narratives inside them, so the purpose of fashion film is to bring out these stories. And frankly, when a designer creates a piece of clothing, he does it for people who move, he imagines how the clothes will look in motion. Fashion film is perfect for showing this dynamic. So arguably, designers have always had their creations compromised by having to show them in still images – even when they were by Irving Penn, Guy Bourdin or Helmut Newton, which were of course great images!

Some of these fashion photographers started to experiment with film already.
That's true. On SHOWstudio we try to show a selection of films from photographers who complemented their work with moving images. Guy Bourdin's fashion films from the 1970s, for example. The interesting thing about them is that they are very simple, but they have all of the values that Bourdin put in his photography. The latent menace, the difficulties with life, the fascination with women and death are all in there – even if sometimes it is just a girl in satin lingerie sitting the wrong way on a revolving chair moving around against a red backdrop. We also came across films by Erwin Blumenfeld, one of the best fashion photographers of all time. He experimented with film as early as in the 1950s, and he showed them to his clients to convince them that they should really be doing moving images. He said: 'To me still image is fine, but actually film is an even better medium for fashion.'

Speaking of Erwin Blumenfeld: is it true that he was the first photographer who started to use black models for magazines?
I don't know about that, to be honest.

He photographed the Afro-American model Bani Yevelston for *Life Magazine* in 1957. But some say that actually the first black model was Adrienne Fidelin, a dancer from Guadeloupe who was Man Ray's girlfriend and who was photographed by Man Ray for *Harper's Bazaar* in 1937.
I think there is not much use in wanting to try to find out exactly which magazine printed the first image of a black model. First you would have to track back when professional modeling started, and you would have to work out and determine when mod-

'The fashion industry is very racist, still is, which is due to the fact that, like most industries, it is controlled by men.'

Still from *Untitled*, a film by Nick Knight and Naomi Campbell for the SHOWstudio project *Political Fashion*, 2008

Model Sarah Wingate wearing Yohji Yamamoto, shot by Nick Knight (1986)

ern fashion photography first started … But I guess you bring it up because I shot a film with Naomi Campbell for SHOWstudio's *Political Fashion* project?

In this film, *Untitled*, you criticize that black models still struggle to find work in the fashion industry. The film shows Naomi Campbell holding two machine guns, shooting blanks directly at the camera.

Naomi certainly liked it! I think she liked the empowering factor. And I liked that the statement of the film was so upfront, you know, almost two-dimensional in a cartoon way. I guess you might wonder why Naomi, of all people, should feel discriminated against – she is very successful after all. But she told me that she hasn't always had a fair deal because of racism and that she didn't get certain jobs because of her skin colour. I do believe her. The fashion industry is very racist, still is, which is due to the fact that, like most industries, it is controlled by men. You have high-powered women editors, but actually the people who pay and make the decisions are men who don't care about equality. All they care about is sales figures and they will make sure to exclude anything that might put these in danger – ending up reinforcing racism and stereotyping people.

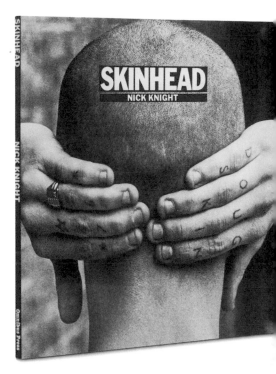

Cover of Nick Knight's *Skinhead* book, published by Omnibus Press in 1982

Does that count for plus-size models as well? The photoshoot you did in 1997 for *i-D* with a nude Sophie Dahl was much discussed at the time.

Well, you always have to lead by example. If you just criticize without offering an alternative culture will never change. I personally believe that curvaceous shapes are just as attractive as so-called ideal body shapes. So whenever I get the chance to photograph somebody who is considered overweight, I have to prove that a curve is just as beautiful and acceptable as a straight line. In fact I have to make my point in a way that people will actually say: 'Oh yeah, I might want to look like that.'

So fashion can really have political impact?

How could fashion not be political? I think a lot of people have a problem acknowledging it – they think fashion is transient and changing all the time while they expect political thought to be constant and leading to permanency. But what we learn today is that politics can change even quicker than fashion! Besides, fashion and clothes are our first means of communication. What we wear always makes a statement about who we are, what we stand for and what we believe in. Class difference, sexual availability, maturity – all these signals are given out by way of dressing. So fashion is very political! I had all these things written all over myself in my late teens when I was a skinhead …

Lady Gaga, shot by Nick Knight for the September 2010 issue of *Vanity Fair*

You documented this time in your life in your very first book, *Skinhead*, published in 1982.

Yes, being a skinhead was an enormous pathway of me realizing the effect clothes have. I got involved in skinheadism for very personal reasons. I grew up in Belgium and France because my father was in the diplomatic corps of NATO. So when I got back to Britain in 1970, my fashion codes were completely different, I looked like I'd come straight from Mars. At the time skinheadism was a huge cult in Britain, and I was looking for a place to fit in. And then at 15 I found myself falling in love with a girl next door who was a skinhead ... Of course there was also a deliberate provocation of the intellectual background I had. My mother was a psychotherapist, we were very middle-class and I was brought up very liberally. So there was a desire to reject everything that I had been told at home and to engage with something I knew was wrong – but I think that is how we perform ourselves with people when we are teenagers.

How would you describe your take on cosmetic surgery?

I am all for it! I really don't have any problem with people having cosmetic surgery or changing their bodies. Maybe it's because I studied biology? I really would have loved to be able to photograph Michael Jackson, for example. Before he died, I would get a phone call from somebody's office every so often, saying 'Could you photograph Michael Jackson for this magazine or this project?' I said 'Yes, I'd love to!' every time, but then it never quite happened. What a pity! Actually one of the projects that we had on SHOWstudio was about this topic – bodies and the ways of changing them, as represented through fashion.

You mean facelifts, diet pills, botox and muscle building?

Exactly. Our project *The Fashion Body* was looking at male fashion designers and the ways their bodies are quite strange. You know, fashion designers have always changed women's shapes, but they never really took it on themselves. But now they start to be very creative with their bodies – look at Marc Jacobs, who became sort of addicted to the gym after his rehab, or Karl Lagerfeld, who went from one shape to a completely different shape. I would never criticize the body-styling industry or make fun of cosmetic surgery. These techniques offer highly fascinating possibilites – just as any new Photoshop tool is fascinating, or any new 3D printer. What is crucial is what you do with it. I don't think people should be made to feel they have to alter their body because anything is wrong with them and they should conform to certain ideals. Instead we should aim to use those techniques to diversify our notions of beauty and do something really interesting and imaginative.

Otherwise all people would end up looking the same and ultimately there would be no more exceptional beauty?

That would be terrible! I don't see why we always have to straighten or downsize our noses. We could make them bigger. And instead of liposuction, bolstering up or smoothing, we could allow ourselves to be inspired by animals. I'm sure it won't be long before we will be medically able to change all sorts of things. Let's have a chameleon skin that changes colour from blue to red! Actually, I would like to have the muscles and the front teeth of a leopard. It would be much more sexually attractive!

Iris van HERPEN

">*FASHION DESIGNER*
Amsterdam

The techniques and formal language employed by Iris van Herpen are often culled from outside the field of fashion – and that's precisely why her dresses reflect the essence of fashion itself. Born in Wamel, Holland, in 1984, the designer studied at the ArtEZ Kunsthochschule Arnheim and completed an internship with Alexander McQueen before launching her own Amsterdam-based label in 2007. Van Herpen's couture creations are sculptural masterpieces, products of weeks of manual craft- ing or of a laser beam that melts and shapes layer upon layer of synthetic polymer in a 3D printer. *Time Magazine* rated one of her 3D dresses among the 50 best creations of 2011, and she became an honorary member of the venerable Chambre Syndicale de la Haute Couture in Paris that same year. Van Herpen launched a prêt-à-porter collection in 2013.

Iris van Herpen, what do you make of the term 'science fashion'? It comes up frequently when writers try to put your work into words.
Well, the term certainly does stick in your head, but I would never call my work 'science fashion' myself. I'm not a scientist. For some of my dresses I use technologies that
are new to fashion, and some people might describe them as futuristic, for example 3D
printing – but that doesn't make me a scientist. Most of my dresses are still made by
hand, using pure craft. It's not like they materialize in some sort of sterile laboratory.
And to be honest, when I think about 'science fashion', I don't like the reference to science fiction at all …

There is a fictional quality to your dresses.
Of course, there is fantasy in them, but not in a clichéd retro-futurist sense. By fantasy
I mean imagination in its true sense. When I imagine a dress, the practical part is not
the first thing that comes to my mind – which can turn into quite a challenge when
I actually *make* the dress. Reality is just that one very simple perspective to hold on to
for people to not get insane. I admire people who are smart enough to not get stuck in
this one reality but create their own. For example, if you look at women like Björk or
Daphne Guinness …

… both of whom love wearing your dresses …
They are not afraid to *be*, they have created their own beautiful reality. They dare to
show their own perspective on the world, which is inspiring to see.

You draw on knowledge from outside the world of fashion as strongly as possible and engage in dialogues with architects, scientists and artists. Is it difficult
not to get carried away by all the information you acquire and keep your focus on
clothes – instead of, say, getting ideas for a new car?
I do have a natural interest in the human body, so mostly when I hear about a new technique or a new material, the idea I get out of it is directly linked to a garment. People
have asked me whether I could design a house or a car, and I don't think I could – not
because I'm not trained for it, but I wouldn't want to work in different fields simultaneously. I believe in specializing. I believe that people – when they strongly focus their
mind on one thing within a lifetime – can create magic at one point. But I also don't
want to get stuck in my own head, and having nothing but fashion in your life doesn't
make you smarter necessarily. That's why I like to inject my work with knowledge from
other disciplines.

What scientific finding has recently fascinated you the most?
Well, I was speaking with Rachel Armstrong, she's a trained architect who's also a biolo-
gist and she has her own laboratory. Through her I have learned about metabolic materials. Rachel is researching materials that are sort of quietly alive. They are not really

alive, of course, but they have a sense so they can react. For example, they can grow and it's possible to control the rate at which they grow.

So using a metabolic fabric, you could potentially create a garment that you start wearing as a child and that grows with you into adulthood?

Maybe that will be possible in the future? For the moment, Rachel is researching these materials in relation to houses, to see how they could self-repair. Houses could actually become a part of nature, instead of getting damaged by nature through the years. I find that very fascinating, because humankind will have to find ways to work with nature instead of against it. It's the only way to survive.

You mentioned your natural interest in the human body. Does it come from dancing? You trained to be a ballet dancer when you were a teenager.

Yes, classical ballet was my biggest hobby when I was a child, I took four or five hours of lessons per week. In ballet you learn how to control your body and create a special beauty with it. Ballet is transforming the body quite a lot, making it longer, dancing on the toes, things like that. I think fashion is doing the same thing in other ways. People wear heels to appear taller, and in any culture people change their bodies mainly through fashion. So yes, for me, dancing was really the beginning of my fascination for the body, its functionality and its shapes.

Dancers need to understand movement in space. Many fashion designers don't really work that way. Instead they sketch their ideas on paper, which is a process in two dimensions.

It's true, dancing really made me think in 3D. That's the reason why I can't draw my ideas that well. On paper they don't look the same as in my head. Reducing something to 2D, then making it 3D again – I think it's a weird and limiting process. Instead of drawing a lot, I much prefer to work with materials directly, moulding them and wrestling with them.

Would it be wrong to say that your familiarity with ballet also shows in the sense of tension and flexibility in a lot of your dresses? For instance, in a dress from your autumn/winter 2011 collection Capriole, you use the internal tension of leather straps to create nice bow shapes that are perfectly balanced, flexible but also firm.

As I said, ballet is about finding ultimate control over the body, and I think within my work as a designer my goal is to find ultimate control over the material. I'm really a material freak, I love fighting with materials. It's almost like a meditation for me. In the beginning, when you start working with a material, it's always the material saying what it wants to do. But if you really focus on it and do it over and over again, at some point you start leading the conversation.

Another example would be a white coat from your spring/summer 2013 collection Voltage, which looks like it's made from paper, with amazing structures of big squares that resemble origami folds.

That piece was made from a very light but very strong technical material that the architect Philip Beesley has introduced me to. The material is super thin and it's laser cut, and Philip has balanced out the shape so well – cutting it a little bit shorter here, and then a little bit longer there – that it just stands out and holds itself. It's really a miracle structurally!

Mirror dress from the *Voltage* collection backstage at Iris van Herpen's haute couture show in Paris in January 2013

You rarely work with plain, smooth surfaces, instead you often construct surfaces from accumulations of smaller surfaces, using the shapes of bulges, strings,
spokes and such. Why?

Assembling surfaces from different shapes and structures creates an interaction between them – so it's not only about one piece itself, but also about the space in between
its parts. It's a sort of language, how they connect with each other and how they react on
each other. I also think that structures are much more interesting haptically than plain
surfaces. I myself like to wear something that triggers my tactile sense with a structure
that I can play with.

As a fashion student you interned with Alexander McQueen. What interested you
in his work at the time?

As a student, looking at his work, I was fascinated by his outstanding craftsmanship
and the complexity of it all. You know, in a lot of garments you can sort of see exactly
how they are made, but with a lot of McQueen's designs you just couldn't. You were
left wondering how it's possible to achieve that sort of layering, that shape or light-
ness with a particular material. For me, that was the trigger, because as a student you
learn all sorts of techniques, but you need to find your own way of piecing them
together.

And the man himself?

I was fascinated by him, of course. He seemed to have found his own handwriting, a
signature that he really stuck to. I respect that a lot, when people just go for their own
thing and don't listen too much to what the rest of the fashion world thinks.

*'I think that
structures are
much more
interesting
haptically than
plain surfaces.
I myself like
to wear
something
that triggers my
tactile sense.'*

At the *Voltage* show in January 2013; pictured left: coat designed in
collaboration with architect Philip Beesley

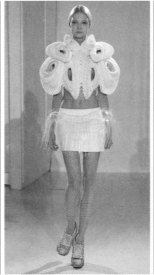

The *Capriole* haute couture show in Paris in July 2011; left: leather strap dress; centre: 3D-printed top; right: dress with 'water splash'

Miguel Adrover, who was friends with him, says that going into partnership with the Gucci Group in 2000 changed a lot for McQueen – it put the market pressure on, so to speak.

I actually heard the same thing from a woman who worked with McQueen for a long time, a seamstress. She said that going into the group changed many things. I guess when a small company becomes part of a really big company, there is a whole different energy, attitude and spirit. I think going through that change must be quite harsh for a designer who started his own brand. But I guess it's also something you are aware of when you choose entering a partnership? Maybe you're not aware of all the consequences …

How about your own business? In 2013 you launched a ready-to-wear collection. How has this affected your work?

Well, I don't have a group telling me how much I have to sell. My company is still quite small and self-owned, I still feel a lot of creative freedom. Of course, launching ready-to-wear means you do want to communicate your work to a larger crowd, but at the same time I really don't have the intention to dress the whole world. I'm not that kind of designer. It's nice that a few more people have access to my creations, but the ready-to-wear hasn't changed my process. Basically I see it as a translation of the things that I explore in haute couture. I couldn't do ready-to-wear without doing couture first.

One assumes that at a certain point launching a ready-to-wear line becomes inevitable for young designers who are trying to keep their business afloat – amazingly intricate couture dresses like yours are probably not very profitable.

It's funny, people tend to think that haute couture is not a market at all, but it is a market, a smaller one of course, but the dresses are also sold at much higher prices. Actually, for a small company like mine launching a ready-to-wear line is riskier, because it means much bigger investments and advance payments. Within haute couture, it's basically just about making one dress at a time. Business-wise that's much less complex. For me, selling dresses to my couture clients and to museums in the last few years has been good enough to pay off the costs and pay my team. But, having said that, it's also nice that I can take the materials and techniques that I sometimes spend weeks or even months experimenting with for the couture and translate them quite quickly into something that is more accessible.

You mentioned 3D printing earlier. You're one of the first fashion designers to work with this technique. Do you think that someday people will simply print out their outfits at home, every morning a new one?

To be honest, I don't think we will see everybody having their own 3D printer at home anytime soon. 3D printing is becoming a new technique for fashion, yes, but I assume it will always be quite expensive. I imagine there to be 3D printing factories where you can order a dress and have it delivered to your home. Anyway, for printing a dress you will always need a machine that is at least twice as big as the dress itself. That's not very practical for home use …

In an interview with SHOWstudio you said that the possibilities of 3D printing also often give you ideas to try out new techniques by hand.

That's true. Sometimes when I'm trying to find out how I can create a certain structure, working with a 3D print really opens up my mind and suddenly gives me an idea which other material I could use and how I could handle it – so 3D printing really inspires my hand work.

Interestingly, the resulting dresses often look like fossils, as if they came from a pre-historic time long before fashion and technology existed. They symbolically span thousands of years of culture and evolution – which basically provokes the question: what is your understanding of time?

Interesting question. When I design I'm not trying to design another time or go into another time or anything like that. It's more that I completely lose sense of time. When I'm really into my work, I'm in a state of mind that is not related to daily things. That's a really nice feeling because time is influencing everything around us so much, you know, the fastness of everything. I'm happy when I'm in this rare moment where there is no time. And if you really think about it: time is so abstract anyway, it doesn't really exist. It's a concept, created to measure infinity, or whatever you want to call it. Time is like a religion, everybody just believes in it.

So in this sense one might see fashion – with its six-months cycles of new collections, new looks and innovations – as one of the means created to experience and make palpable the fiction of time?

Something like that, maybe. But of course, fashion today is not about six-months cycles anymore, most brands work in three-months cycles, or even faster, with all the resort collections in between. Actually fashion has accelerated so much that there is no time to appreciate what is being created anymore. It's insane. Sometimes I wonder when people still find the time to look around and be inspired?

At the *Voltage* show; this 3D-printed dress was designed in collaboration with the Austrian architect Julia Koerner and produced by the Belgian 3D manufacturer Materialise.

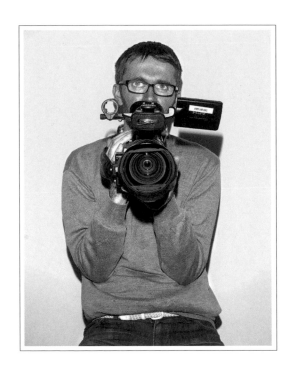

Loïc PRIGENT

DOCUMENTARY FILM-MAKER
Paris

Loïc Prigent is the leading contemporary maker of documentary films about the world of fashion – an expert who does not succumb to the lure of glamour and excitement but instead probes more deeply in order to understand exactly what people are doing and *how* they do it. Prigent's television documentaries, *Signé Chanel* (2005) and *Marc Jacobs & Louis Vuitton* (2007), are legendary, as is *The Day Before*, his series – launched in 2009 – which documents the last 36 hours prior to shows put on by leading fashion houses like Lanvin, Gaultier and Rykiel. Born in Landivisiau in Brittany in 1973, the journalist's first film focused on music: in the mid-1990s, Prigent captured Daft Punk at a concert in Birmingham very early in their career, before the duo began wearing helmets. The material remains a well-kept secret – not a single second of the film has ever been posted on YouTube.

Monsieur Prigent, you don't necessarily look like a fashionista. Jeans, sweatshirt, three-day stubble ... It's more the look of a student.

Maybe. What are you getting at?

Does this look work as an advantage for you when you film documentaries in haute couture houses?

No, I wouldn't say that. People who dress like circus monkeys are embraced by fashion designers all the more. In fashion, people do like it when others dress daringly, you know. But on the other hand, I guess when we film the seamstresses in the ateliers, the so-called *petites mains*, it's better not to look like a freak show. They might be irritated by that, because sometimes we film them for weeks while they work on the same dress, and they are not allowed to wear anything but simple white aprons. In any case, my look is not calculated.

Since your five-part documentary Signé Chanel, finished in 2005, you're regarded as one of the best contemporary fashion film-makers. What is your background?

You mean what I studied? I didn't really study. I come from the countryside, from Britanny. My parents were running holiday houses there, so I spent my summers as a tourist guide for German families. I was surrounded by nothing but artichokes and my only contact with the outside world were magazines. I bought them in stacks – fashion magazines like *i-D*, *The Face* or *Harper's Bazaar*. That was before the internet arrived, you know.

In what way were these magazines important for your career?

I gobbled them up like novels. All those stories about new designers and their careers, how they rise and fall ... It all seemed very glamourous to me, so cruel and over the top, a bit like in *Dallas*. Only that this was about fashion, not oil. And it was really happening! I became quite obsessive with magazines and started publishing my own fanzines. People in Paris read them. They offered me to write for them. So at 19, I started contributing to the newspaper *Libération*, writing on pop and youth culture. Then I got some fashion gigs during Fashion Week, and it all grew from there.

In one episode of your documentary The Day Before, Sonia Rykiel says that she always loved reading your texts on fashion. She thinks you're a very good writer ...

Well, it's also due to my writing that I work for television today. My texts were noticed by people at Canal+, and they convinced me to come and work for their shows.

Would you say today that television is the better medium for reporting on fashion compared to newspapers and magazines?

That's a difficult question. On the one hand, no, because it's very hard to have fashion projects green-lighted in television. Even in France – although it's such a fashion country – the bosses of television channels are almost always straight guys who only like soccer and who couldn't care less about fashion. On the other hand, television – or the moving image in general – seems better suited to make a statement about fashion. At

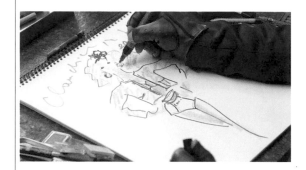

'Did you know that, until recently, there was actually a law in France still forbidding women to wear pants?'

Top right and centre left:
Karl Lagerfeld in *Karl Lagerfeld se dessine* (2013); bottom left:
Loïc Prigent films Karl Lagerfeld in *The Day Before: Fendi by Karl Lagerfeld* (2009); centre right: still from *The Day Before: Sonia Rykiel* (2009)

least there is often a problem with fashion writing: many writers tend to put a lot of psychology in what they see that isn't really there.

Is that your own experience, too?

Of course. I was in New York once to see a fashion show and the catwalk was a triangle of cement which they had wetted. A wet triangle … you get it? It's obvious! But when I talked to the designers about the sexual allusion, they had never thought of it! But of course journalists, especially writers for newspapers and magazines, want to read meaning into this because … well, they have to write about *something*. Even when reading about Yves Saint Laurent, I sometimes think: isn't this a bit over-interpreted? You know, in retrospect Yves Saint Laurent is mostly portrayed as a genius …

In France, Saint Laurent is a national hero!

Well, yes. But one reason for this is that his lover and business partner Pierre Bergé has hijacked the collective memory of French fashion, in terms of keeping everything Saint Laurent ever did – every drawing, every letter, every photograph is archived and well preserved. It's different with Hubert de Givenchy, who always destroyed everything.

In your film *Yves Saint Laurent: The Last Fashion Show,* you document Saint Laurent's retirement show from 2002. In the film, Pierre Bergé emphasizes that Saint Laurent was never about fashion, but about style. What's your take on this statement?

Actually, I have asked a lot of people who knew Saint Laurent how he was, and apparently he could talk about scarves and belts for whole nights. So I guess he really was a fashion guy! But in a way, Pierre Bergé's statement holds true. When you look at Saint Laurent's last show, a lot of the dresses are not passé. They could be on the runway tomorrow. The black blazers are completely timeless. *Le Smoking* was never about setting a trend, but about defining a style for the working woman who dares to wear pants. Did you know that there was actually a law in France still forbidding women to wear pants? It was from 1800 and repealed only recently. The French government was looking through stupid old laws and they discovered that it was still on the books!

One of the most fascinating sequences in your Saint Laurent documentary is about the famous Mondrian dresses from 1965 – dresses that seemed to be demystified completely by countless reproductions in books and magazines. But after watching your film they seem even more mysterious …

I know! Fashion is full of marvellous details that you don't notice at first sight. First of all, everybody thinks that the colours of the Mondrian dresses were different fabrics vulgarly sewn together. But actually the Mondrian dress is made from one piece of fabric! And the colours are not printed, it's much more complicated. Apparently it's an intricate embroidery. I imagine it to be something like the vitrail technique for church windows … but I'm not sure myself! And then when you see the footage of the models wearing the dresses, you notice that the fabric of the shoulder doesn't touch the actual skin of the model. So there must be some kind of really intricate shoulder pad in there – which you don't see if you only look at a picture. My guess is that the Mondrian dresses were actually too easy for the ateliers to make – you know, it's really only a piece of fabric with three holes in it. So maybe the people in the ateliers were insulted that they should make something that simple and they would challenge themselves and say: 'Okay, let's do this really complicated!'

Are the fashion houses in which you film never afraid that the beautiful mystery of their brand might be harmed once a camera enters their ateliers?

Well, fashion houses have always been very secretive. They usually try to control everything – images, press releases, reviews, etc. But the more effort you put in regulating your image, the bigger the danger of being considered a fake. I think that's why they agree to let me in. They want to show that their products are not just about marketing but actually the result of a lot of skilled craft and hard work.

Since the advent of mobile phones with cameras, it is impossible to control the circulation of images anyway. There have been YouTube videos shot by models backstage at a Chanel show that were actually quite embarrassing for Chanel.

I know. Well, the houses want to open their doors a little bit more – but not too much of course. They don't want the mystery to disappear! So I'm a perfect match in a way. I'm not interested in gossip, I'm not Twitter. If I film someone saying 'Shit! Fuck! Shit!' and they ask me right away not to use the footage, I won't. I still like a good drama of course, but I'm not there to be sadistic in my filming of the ateliers.

For Signé Chanel you were even allowed to install a surveillance camera above the coffee vending machine in the Maison Chanel …

Yes, I wanted to find out what happens in front of the machine during the final days before a show. It was really a bit like in *Big Brother*. But, you know, you only get good footage if you really film everything – you can select afterwards. I never stop filming. I often see my colleagues from television entering backstage at a fashion show and they are disappointed because they don't see the things they expect right away. They want to film the designer having temper tantrums and they want everybody snorting cocaine. They are frustrated if they don't get these images immediately. They say, 'Oh, we have nothing to film here' – while right in front of them there is a woman doing beautiful embroidery! My experience is that you never get the material you expect. That's why we start filming early in the mornings when work in the ateliers starts, and if they add a nightshift to finish the dresses, we stay, too – and film how they pin needles in their fingers from fatigue.

Selecting and editing the material must be a nightmare.

Of course! But this is also the only way to win people's trust. Karl Lagerfeld, for example, was quite surprised when I never left his side while filming *Signé Chanel*. He had assumed I would film him only ten minutes per day. But when he realized I was serious about this, he became more friendly. And when he noticed how very friendly the directresses from the ateliers were with me, he became even friendlier!

Lagerfeld seems to really have taken a liking to you since. In 2013, he even agreed to sketch his own biography for you in Karl Lagerfeld Draws Himself.

It took me two years to convince him of the idea. In the film, he's reviewing his whole life in sketches and you hear him talking about them. No archive footage, only him drawing. It's amazing how Karl can recapture any moment of his life in a sketch that's snappy and full of life within 20 seconds. Some of his drawings were social comments

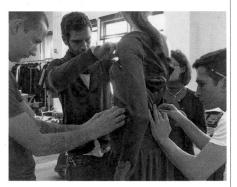

Top row: stills from *The Day Before: Lanvin* (2011); second row: still from *The Day Before: Proenza Schouler* (2009); third row: Donatella Versace in *The Day Before: Donatella Versace* (2010); bottom row left: Diane von Furstenberg in *The Day Before: Diane von Furstenberg* (2010); bottom row right: Marc Jacobs in *Marc Jacobs & Louis Vuitton* (2007)

Stills from *The Day Before: Jean Paul Gaultier* (2009, top) and *The Day Before: Sonia Rykiel* (2009, below)

on Paris in the 50s, some of them show people, impressions, places, himself … even Jacques de Bascher, who was the love of his life. Karl made three drawings of him for the film!

Are there any fashion documentaries or fashion films that have inspired you in terms of camera techniques, dramatization or cut?

There are a few documentaries about artisans, for example *Le sabotier du Val de Loire* from 1956. It's the first documentary the French director Jacques Demy did, before he became famous with *The Young Girls of Rochefort*. It is a short film about a guy who makes wooden clogs, and it's amazing to see the amount of work that goes into these shoes and the centuries-old tools the man uses. That film is a landmark to me. And concerning the dramatization of fashion on screen, I think William Klein's *Qui êtes-vous, Polly Maggoo?* from 1966 is still unequalled – especially the scene in which the fashion editor gets up at the end of the fashion show to give her verdict: 'Hallelujah!'

A person who doesn't know that *Qui êtes-vous, Polly Maggoo?* is actually a satire on the career of a model in Paris might take the film for a documentary.

Yes, to me it *is* a documentary! The way William Klein depicts the fashion show in the film: these are documentary images. He couldn't have made up images like that. In fact, shortly before he shot *Polly Maggoo*, Klein went to fashion shows in Paris in the 60s. He filmed a Saint Laurent show for *Dim, Dam, Dom*, which was a quite revolutionary

French television show for women at the time. So Klein knew what was going on in fashion. That's why the fashion images he staged for *Qui êtes-vous, Polly Maggoo?* are as iconic as a magazine spread, even today.

Polly Maggoo is said to have been influential on 60s' fashion: the aluminium dresses that were custom-made for the film by the artists François and Bernard Baschet allegedly inspired Paco Rabanne's and André Courrèges's legendary metal fashion.

Who inspires whom? Who steals, who creates? These are always interesting questions, but in fashion it is hardly possible to answer them precisely.

In your film *Marc Jacobs & Louis Vuitton,* the answer is easy. We see Marc Jacobs in Japan, where he meets the artist Yayoi Kusama, whom he adores. Dotted patterns are Kusama's trademark – and Jacobs' new designs for Vuitton are full of dots. Jacobs even jokes about it in his atelier. When an employee asks him about his meeting with Kusama, he says: 'She's dotty.'

That may be an embarrasing moment for Marc Jacobs, but he doesn't care. He's an ironic guy who's not at all about being polished all the time. I love that about him. Before I followed him with my camera, he hadn't let a single television team come near him. But when I filmed him, he never hesitated one second to put himself on his knees to adjust a dress with pins in his mouth. When he came to see the finished film before it was aired, he cried. I think it was really touching for him when his friend, the painter Elizabeth Peyton, explains why she thinks that he's an artist: because only an artist could mould the world according to his imagination so that the streets are full of young girls wearing violet velvet pants and sequined ballerina shoes. That moved him deeply, because I think he secretly wants to be an artist, too.

The day after you finished shooting your documentary in March 2007, Marc Jacobs checked into rehab. There's not a single scene hinting at a drug problem in your film ...

I know that Marc Jacobs went into rehab shortly after, but the exact next day? I doubt that. He would have told me about it, he would have enjoyed saying straight into the camera: 'I am going to rehab because they're sending me there.' Actually he was in very good shape the last time I filmed him. He had just started this new treatment for his health, he drank mangostan and goji juice before his lunch and he took Omega-3 pills and VSL 3 powder. You see it in the film.

Are there any designers who keep refusing your requests to document their work?

Alber Elbaz at Lanvin refused for years until I finally got him for my series *The Day Before*. He always said he was afraid of the camera and that it would disturb his process. It's funny, he only agreed to be filmed after I showed one of my documentaries in Israel at a fashion festival in Holon, where he grew up. At the Q&A, after the screening, somebody asked me 'Who do you want to film?' and I said 'Alber Elbaz! I always tell him: Alb*er* rhymes with documen*taire*.' Apparently his niece was there and she told him about it. So I think he was touched by that. And I also tried to get Nicolas Ghesquière while he was still at Balenciaga, but they refused several times. I'm so pissed! Nobody has documented his process there and his work with the ateliers. It's really a shame ...

Barbara *VINKEN*

FASHION THEORIST

Munich

Although fashion is not her primary field, she is always on the mark when she discusses it. Born in Hanover, Germany, in 1960, Barbara Vinken is Professor of Romance and Comparative Literatures at the University of Munich. Her book *Mode nach der Mode. Kleid und Geist am Ende des 20. Jahrhunderts* (1993) has become a standard work in the field of fashion theory, and was published in English under the title *Fashion Zeitgeist* in 2005. In this book, Vinken examines the rhetoric of fashion from Lagerfeld to Comme des Garçons, and chronicles the demise of classical haute couture. Vinken has observed a gradual restoration of the ideal of elegance – as exemplified by Lanvin, among others – since the turn of the millennium.

Co-author: Philipp Ekardt

There are two reasons, or actually three. The first is that France has been the land of fashion for several centuries. Until the 1980s, Paris was the undisputed capital of fashion. In the 17th and 18th centuries, the French court was considered to be *the* place where fashion took place. And so any scholar of Romance languages who studies the literature and culture of France must also dedicate some thought to fashion. The second reason is that I am, as a literature expert, fascinated by fashion because I think that one can read clothes in the same way as one reads a poem.

Could you elaborate on that?

When scholars study fashion, they generally do so from a sociological point of view. I felt that it was important to move away from this approach and to work towards an aesthetic view of fashion. One could also say: a formalist view of fashion. The things that I deal with daily in the study of literature – the crossing of horizons of understanding, connotation, association, intertextuality, and so on – can certainly also be examined with reference to clothes. However, nobody had done that systematically until I wrote my book *Fashion Zeitgeist*. In fact, the link is this: text – texture – textile. And that works very well. The third reason is that I simply love clothes. A very trivial, emotional reason.

This last point becomes very clear in *Fashion Zeitgeist*, a book in which you approach your subject with the instruments of literary theory, but not in order to merely produce an extended 'textual semiology'. Rather, your analysis is thoroughly informed by a very elaborate and even technical sartorial vocabulary. This shows, for example, in your description of an evening dress by Comme des Garçons, in which you take apart its patterning, talk about how seams are stitched, and so on.

Yes, I've acquainted myself with these things, as well as with the vocabulary that goes with them.

Did you go to fashion school? Did it run in the family?

There is indeed a degree of familial predisposition: my mother worked as a designer. She designed stockings, in the Rhineland, for KuAG in Waldniel. There were still a great number of textile factories at the time, which have all been forced to close down since. My mother designed for them.

You just spoke of Paris as the capital of fashion in the past tense. *Fashion Zeitgeist* is an attempt to analyse this transition, i.e. to analyse the end of the haute couture period in the 1980s, which also marked the rise of deconstructive designers such as Comme des Garçons and Martin Margiela. Could you describe

Barbara Vinken in a Lanvin dress at home

where fashion finds itself today, more than 20 years later?
Maybe I should begin by pointing out that the German title of my book translates as 'fashion after fashion', and one could indeed say that we have now arrived in the era after 'fashion after fashion'. I mean that in two senses. First, for some time now, there has been a strong renaissance of Paris as the capital of fashion. Secondly, we now have a form of fashion setting the tone again that incorporates the subversive, ironic tendencies that characterized Comme des Garçons and Martin Margiela, but at the same time it places renewed emphasis on elegance and classic body contouring. If you look, for example, at the collections designed by Nicolas Ghesquière for Balenciaga, or Alber Elbaz's celebrated clothes for Lanvin, it becomes clear that they are also about a restoration of a French, continental idea of fashion. Elbaz and Ghesquière, as well as companies such as Chloé and Givenchy, integrate rhetorical figures that were invented by the radical fashion of the 1980s – open seams, asymmetry, an emphasis on fasteners, and so on – in a highly sophisticated manner. They lay bare everything that used to be hidden in haute couture, in a way that is similar to what 'fashion after fashion' did. But they tone down these tendencies once again; they are no longer as radical as they were with Rei Kawakubo and Margiela. I would call this a restoration of the ideal of elegance.

This also relates to the fact that Nicolas Ghesquière is celebrated for being 'a real dressmaker', whereby being a dressmaker is certainly no longer the only route to becoming a successful designer.
That's right. However, the couturiers of 'fashion after fashion', such as Kawakubo and Margiela, always emphasized that they were dressmakers, too. But the clothes they made of course had a particular sort of irony and aggression.

Would you agree that the fashion of the early 2000s was characterized mainly by a very strong reference to the styles of subcultures? Hedi Slimane might be the paradigmatic example of this.
Not really, because this idea is a very old one. It was even applied by Coco Chanel. Chanel used fine cotton rib, one of the cheapest fabrics for workers, and turned it into high fashion. The twist and dissonance achieved by taking materials from street wear or, for example, the proletarian classes, and ennobling it – or doing the reverse, by devaluing precious materials – these moves were part of haute couture from the very beginning. This did not – as has often been claimed – start with Yves Saint Laurent in the 1960s. One might even say that the use of street wear in haute couture ended with Yves Saint Laurent, although of course Vivienne Westwood later did this to great effect again.

Is fashion today – as classic haute couture and also 'fashion after fashion' used to be – still concerned with gender relations at all? Or is the fact that menswear designers like Tom Ford and Hedi Slimane have a much greater impact actually an indication that men can now be objects of fashion just as easily as women?

That's a difficult question. If bourgeois fashion differentiates between fashion for women as marked erotic fashion and fashion for men as non-marked erotic fashion, the increasingly prominent homosexual culture and the phenomenon of metrosexuality certainly indicate that the conditions have become much more fluid. Fashion for men that aggressively marks erotic qualities may not yet be mainstream, but it is definitely much more visible and noticeable than it used to be. Karl Lagerfeld even has a male muse in the model Baptiste Giabiconi, and of course he stages him accordingly – as one might expect from Lagerfeld.

In *Fashion Zeitgeist,* you point out that fashion did not become 'fashion' in the present-day sense until women were forbidden to wear trousers, as professed by Rousseau, in 1793, and men were no longer permitted to pretty up. Fashion from then onwards was only for women.

Yes, I described fashion as a post-feudal phenomenon in the sense that after the French Revolution, the women of the increasingly powerful bourgeoisie adopted the erotic displays of the aristocracy, whereas the eroticism of men had to remain unmarked from then onwards. This was a substantial change. Until then, both men and women had flaunted their charms in fashion. The display of the male leg was central.

The muscular calf was a symbol of strength and virility.

Exactly. The male leg was appealingly displayed in sheer silk stockings, higher than in any miniskirt. Or just think of the codpiece in Baroque fashion. The male sex, like the leg, was emphasized as an extremely erotic signal. This was no longer the case in bourgeois fashion. The emphasis on the male body ceased and was shifted entirely to women. Perhaps the reintroduction of the codpiece through Gaultier was in this respect another turning point, even if it was, of course, a joke.

Even if the male body is once again more emphatically eroticized, this does not mean that we have returned to living in feudal times?

Of course not. In feudal times the main difference did not, as in bourgeois times, lie in sex – male or female – but in class boundaries that separated people: the aristocracy versus the common people, the upper classes against the lower classes. However, it looks as though we might be moving in that direction again, towards a society in which class and descent are more important than sex. At least we have proper robber barons again, as there were in the Middle Ages, with the law on their side.

As a scholar of Romance literature, could you say what has become of the fashion novel? In the 19th century, there was an entire tradition of the fashion novel, not least Flaubert's *Madame Bovary*.

That's a good question. I can't see an equivalent today. In Germany there is a writer who does write a lot about fashion in his novels: Thomas Meinecke. He describes clothing in great detail. But apart from him …?

'One should point out that H&M imitates on a primitive level the very processes that were developed by Karl Lagerfeld.'

Fashion books in Barbara Vinken's apartment

Maybe celebrity culture has taken the place of the fashion novel? Doesn't the life of Victoria Beckham, for example, function something like a real-life fashion novel, with her various surgical procedures and all of her suffering of desperately wanting to look like a top model?

In terms of the celebrity thing, I wonder whether its influence on fashion might not be greatly exaggerated. There have always been style icons. Sissi was a style icon, Marie Antoinette, and Jackie Kennedy, too. They didn't dress themselves, either. They were dressed by others and kitted out by designers. In this respect, the differentiation between the style icons of the past – who determined their own styles – and present-day celebrities – who simply wear whatever they are given – isn't accurate, either. The narcissistic element is definitely increased by the fact that, today, celebrities are always immediately on display. Whatever they do, there are photographs and videos of it. In this respect, one could say that celebrity culture has always existed, and the only difference today lies in our constant exposure to its presence in the media, which results in a stronger appeal to narcissism.

What is your take on the trend of cross-branding? Karl Lagerfeld has designed for H&M, so has Comme des Garçons – two antagonistic fashion positions, joined in cross-branding.

It's true that this model did not exist in the same way in the past. The first thing one should point out here is that H&M imitates on a primitive level the very processes that were developed by Lagerfeld. And then they brought in the original at a later stage – a strategy that borders on the perverse. These instances of designer collaborations are basically a kind of guerrilla concept: the collections are available only for a short time, in very small quantities, and the shops are then virtually stampeded. The desirability is increased to the absolute maximum, not through money – all of a sudden everybody can afford it – but through physical strength or patience. It is, therefore, on the one hand a democratization of luxury in the sense of there being no exclusion anymore, while on the other hand it has the effect of deliberately stimulating desire for a product that has been turned into a fetish. Interestingly, this appears to work even if the designers are not all that famous. Sonia Rykiel, for example, was not known to very many people in Germany. Since she designed underwear for H&M and was plastered all over billboards in every city, she has become well known throughout the country.

Which designers do you personally find most interesting these days?

I find Lanvin very beautiful. I definitely have some restorative tendencies myself in this respect. Alber Elbaz's designs have a light, elegant quality, a hint of nostalgia. Although intellectually, I recognize the weakness, I find it quite prepossessing on an aesthetic level.

Could you give one concrete example?

For a lecture on fashion, I was looking at a cocktail dress from Lanvin's 2009/2010 winter collection. It brings together two hallmarks: first, a thick, sporty zip, and secondly, a ruffle. The zip is Alber Elbaz's signature. He also uses it in cocktail and tulle dresses. The zip thus moves from being a purely functional element to one that is also ornamental. But this ornament, which has primarily military and sporting connotations, carries over its old meaning into the new context, thereby crossing the usual connotations associated with a cocktail dress. As the epitome of feminine elegance and even vulnerability, this stands for the opposite of sporting, masculine functionality. The zip and the ruffle then engage in an intelligent and witty dialogue. The ruffle takes the place of the border, but instead of hiding it in a classic, inconspicuously elegant way, it both conceals and emphasizes the zip in a paradoxical way.

In other words, the dress is an example of the ways in which current Parisian fashion integrates the rhetorical figures that characterized the radical fashion of the 1980s – irony in this particular case?

Precisely. The irony here is further emphasized by the choice of material: the dress is tailored from a simple, blunt wool jersey in which one can move as comfortably as in a tracksuit or a T-shirt. This is not usually the case in evening dresses or cocktail dresses. This means that we encounter here the paradoxical convergence of a number of different connotations. The effect as a whole relies on an aestheticization of the disruptive factor, a harmonization of dissonance, which conveys a contemporary elegance in a witty manner in the form of this dress.

Bookshelves in Barbara Vinken's apartment

Juergen TELLER

FASHION PHOTOGRAPHER
London

Juergen Teller's photographs are known for their hefty humour, but sometimes they can also be very subtle and sensitive. Born in Erlangen, Germany, in 1964, Teller studied at the Bayerische Staatslehranstalt für Photographie in Munich, before moving to London in 1986; there, one of his first assignments was the cover photo for Sinead O'Connor's hit 'Nothing Compares 2 U'. Teller came to fame with his photographs of Nirvana taken during a 1991 tour, as well as with portraits of Kristen McMenamy and Kate Moss. He is married to the London gallerist Sadie Coles and still shoots fashion stories today for magazines such as *032c, Purple* and *Self Service*. Several of the recent past's most iconic ad campaigns – including for Marc Jacobs, Vivienne Westwood and Céline – were Juergen Teller productions.

Mr. Teller, how do you feel about the fact that your aesthetic is often copied?
I don't mind it. Sometimes, when I flip through the usual fashion magazines, I do think: 'That's a bit too much, though.' But what can I do?

A few years ago, for example, there was a Yves Saint Laurent campaign with Kate Moss …
… which wasn't mine! I was the photographer for Yves Saint Laurent campaigns for a while, two years, four seasons. But I didn't have anything to do with this one.

What distinguishes a real Teller from a fake?
The fact that it's real, of course! Let me give you a simple example: if I were to do a completely banal Polaroid shoot with a model standing in front of a white wall, and if I told my assistant or someone else standing close by to take a Polaroid, too, for comparison, then my picture would definitely be the best of the three. That's just the way it is. Because my photographs are always also about me, and about how I position myself in them.

Technically speaking, a real Teller is also characterized by its obtrusive flash and hard shadow, right?
That flash is easy to copy. But I wouldn't say that it is obtrusive or has a brutal effect. My flash really isn't that hard. It just helps to sharpen the pictures, in the sense that it makes them more direct, more intense. What is much more important is that I engage with the people I am taking photographs of.

You mean you take your time to get to know them?
Not necessarily. What matters is that I don't expect the people to do something completely insane in front of the camera. I always respect their character. That's possible even if I only spend a couple of minutes with a person. A lot of photographers are incredibly insensitive in that respect. They don't understand that it is completely pointless to tell a relatively shy, charming man to go wild.

What do you say to these people?
I talk to them. We talk about food, life, about our children, all sorts of things. All the while, I creep up on them like an animal. I usually work with two cameras simultaneously. Holding one in my right hand and the other in my left hand, I take pictures with them alternately. That has an almost hypnotic effect. The other person doesn't know exactly which camera to pay attention to. That really makes people relax!

Do you know whether a photograph is going to work the very moment you press the shutter?
I do know exactly what the photograph will look like, at least.

You used to make a point in interviews of saying that fashion doesn't actually interest you very much.
Those comments have been torn out of context. Of course it is true that I basically stumbled into fashion photography 20 years ago, and that I'm always more interested in the people I take pictures of than I am in what they are wearing. But I am interested

in fashion! For example, I like to play around with a designer's collection and give my imagination free rein with it.

For a while, it seemed as though you had had enough of fashion. Instead of models, you yourself became the preferred subject of your photographs, and the focus was on your naked body rather than on clothes.

Well, I'm not just a fashion photographer. The reason I frequently took pictures of myself for a while was that I had ideas for things that others just didn't want to do. People in the fashion scene can be unbelievably whiny, you know. For example, as soon as I wanted to take photographs in the woods in the winter, they started to moan: 'Oh, it's so cold outside, we can't do that!' This laziness annoyed me so much that I decided to just do it myself. Of course I also wanted to find out what it is like to stand in front of the camera, to open oneself up to the camera.

Quite literally! The entire fashion world knows what your sphincter looks like since you lay on a grand piano, legs up, like a baby whose nappies are being changed, for a photo shoot with the actress Charlotte Rampling, with whom you also shot a Marc Jacobs campaign. Weren't you afraid that you wouldn't get anymore job offers after that?

My agent Katy Baggott was worried about that, but I wasn't. And, interestingly, these photographs have not harmed my career at all. To the contrary: professionally, they have even helped me enormously.

Is that because the people you take photographs of now know exactly what to expect when they meet Juergen Teller? They know what to do in front of your lens?

That's right, people do have a better inkling of the direction I am going to take. They approach it all differently than they did in the past. The stakes have been raised, so to speak.

Speaking of which, did Vivienne Westwood really puke in your studio?

Lots of people have asked me that, but it's funny: that's just sand!

We are talking about a photograph that you took for an autumn/winter campaign for Vivienne Westwood's accessory line. In this picture, Westwood leans forward with a grin on her face, and the pile on the floor in front of her looks like vomit …

The inspiration for this collection was 'Caveman', so it was all about the Stone Age and troglodytes. And so we thought: 'Let's make a little heap of sand on location.' But if people think it is puke: so much the better! Because campaigns always need to attract attention before they can do anything else. Vomit and sand are pretty much the same thing to me, anyway. Both raise questions about advertising and fashion.

What do you mean by that?

If you look at the way handbags are usually advertised in magazines: you see a pretty model holding the handbag up to the camera. And if it's also about the shoes, then her other hand will be holding a shoe towards the camera, too. This incredibly obtuse approach to making ads, this sales pitch, makes me sick. And this revulsion is captured in that picture. Vivienne Westwood and I share the same sense of humour in that respect.

When ads meet humour, there's always the potential for things to go wrong …

Vivienne Westwood, 2007

Of course I essentially tried to do the impossible in this photograph: to make an ad that has the desired positive commercial effect for the label, but that simultaneously casts a critical glance at advertising. That was also true of the Victoria Beckham campaign, by the way.

You stuck Victoria Beckham into a big shopping bag for a Marc Jacobs campaign in 2007.

Exactly. Marc Jacobs and I were thinking: 'What could we do with Victoria Beckham?' After all, the woman herself is a total product. And advertising is all about products. So we said: 'We'll stick her into a shopping bag!'

Victoria Beckham has more of a sense of humour, then, than she is given credit for. In this particular photograph, she sticks her legs out of the bag, one can't see any of her face – the person in the bag could be anybody.

Of course we had to prepare her for the shoot. She didn't come to the studio in L.A. and I told her out of the blue: 'You just hop into that bag and spread your legs.' It took weeks of preparation to convince her to do it. Marc Jacobs explained to her: 'Juergen Teller has been doing my ad campaigns for over ten years now. He has taken pictures of Charlotte Rampling, Cindy Sherman, Meg White and many other stars, and not one of them has ever complained.'

Did it help that you could chat to her about football? You are a big football fan, right?

'If I'm convinced that a campaign is good, it will go to print.'

Daria Werbowy, shot for the Céline campaign, autumn/winter 2012/13

Young Pink Kate, London, 1998

Of course, that did help. I have to say I really am very proud of that photograph. On the one hand, it meets all the requirements of a fashion photograph: the pumps with the pink heels were the most important element of that particular Marc Jacobs collection. They could not have been presented to greater effect in another way.

And simultaneously, you raise the issue of stars prostituting themselves in advertising?

Of course that's ironic. One mustn't forget the power of the smiley effect. That smile is even suggested by the string on the bag ...

Have you ever gone too far in a campaign, in the sense that it was rejected by the client?

No. It did happen once that the Marc Jacobs people didn't want to use a picture I had selected. It was for a men's campaign: the American director Harmony Korine is holding a little black girl in his arms. They didn't like that.

Were the Marc Jacobs people concerned about paedophilia?

No. Strangely enough, they thought the picture could be interpreted as racist. None of us could see why, neither my agent, nor my wife, nor I. But we simply used another picture. The girl is in that picture, too, but Harmony isn't holding her. With that exception, up until now everything has been well received. If I'm convinced that a campaign is good, it will go to print.

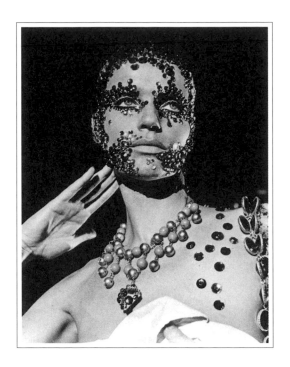

VERUSCHKA

MODEL AND ARTIST
Berlin

Veruschka has gone down in history as one of the first supermodels, even if the word had not yet been invented. Born in Königsberg, East Prussia, in 1939, Countess Vera von Lehndorff-Steinort was a regular *Vogue* cover girl throughout the 1960s, when the 1.83-metre-tall young lady with mysterious, pallid, bluish-grey eyes was avidly pursued by photographers like Richard Avedon, Peter Beard and Franco Rubartelli. Her five-minute cameo in Antonioni's film *Blow-up* (1966) remains legendary to this day. Veruschka, whose father, Count Heinrich Graf von Lehndorff-Steinort, was executed as a participant in the 1944 Stauffenberg plot to assassinate Adolf Hitler, has since the 1970s presented herself (and her body) as a performance artist.

Mrs. von Lehndorff, what is beauty?
Please, let's do without the 'von'. My aristocratic name means absolutely nothing to me.

All right, Vera Lehndorff, what is beauty?
Of course that can't be explained in just a few words. Beauty can only be perceived where there is more than mere appearance. Beauty is that which touches and attracts, but it also means different things to different people. The film director Paul Morrissey once told me that he thought I looked as beautiful as a *Vogue* cover the first time he saw me. To me, that didn't feel like a compliment at all! After all, we all know what matters when it comes to *Vogue* covers: they have to sell. Nothing else. What has that got to do with beauty?

In the 1960s, you were often on the cover of *Vogue*.
Yes, but of all of those covers, I like only a single one now; one that's quite different from all the others. Models usually have to beam on the covers of magazines and look full of *joie de vivre*. Or at least that was the case at the time …

'Up!'
Exactly. How boring! On this cover, however, I'm looking into the distance with a melancholy expression. I have no idea how we were able to get away with it at that time. Diana Vreeland, who was then editor-in-chief of American *Vogue*, only ever really wanted to see one expression on the cover, and that was direct and happy. I assume that the only reason why the cover wasn't stopped was that the photograph had been taken by the famous Richard Avedon. That was during Vreeland's crazy time; she gave us a great deal of freedom.

Such as?
Oh, I could ring her in the middle of the night and say: 'Diana, I've had an idea: I want to take photographs by the sea in the reeds, with gold jewellery that sparkles through the reeds.' She thought that was great! She then sent me to the *Vogue* jewellery department and told me I should take whatever I liked. The photographer Franco Rubartelli and I then drove to the sea, just the two of us, without an assistant, and took the pictures there. And everything was printed exactly as it was. That would no longer be possible these days! It also happened that Vreeland phoned me in the middle of the night, simply to tell me that she had just seen the most beautiful photograph of a horse. She would rhapsodize about its mane for hours: 'It's maaarvelous!' That's

how she talked. Vreeland could go absolutely crazy about some picture or a particular colour.

She was also said to be very strict.

Oh yes, I wouldn't have wanted to be her employee. If she didn't like something, she really let her employees have it. Vreeland was, after all, famous for handing out slaps first thing in the morning in the studio when she was still a stylist, in the 1940s and 1950s, to make the poor models' cheeks look rosier.

Vreeland must have liked Veruschka for being an artificial character.

Nobody knew that at the time; I never told anybody.

Vreeland was herself an artificial character – she found the truth incredibly boring. She is often quoted as saying: 'Never say what is true, it's too boring.'

You are absolutely right. To me, she said: 'Veruschka, never say where you were born.' She suggested that I tell people I come from somewhere on the border between Poland, Russia and Germany; that sounded much more dramatic than 'East Prussia.'

So Veruschka came from the Cold War front, and dressed exclusively in existential black.

That is why I made such a strong impression on the photographers from the very beginning. In the 1960s, there weren't any Russian models in America yet. So that was always part of my performances: Eastern Europe, Communism, and the construction of the Berlin Wall. Veruschka was a mysterious figure. It had been quite different during my first sojourn in New York in 1960: then, I was just Vera from Germany, and nobody was interested in me.

So the Veruschka strategy worked.

Absolutely. When I went to America for the second time in 1961, I worked out exactly what I would look like as Veruschka, how I would walk, how I would enter a room and what my answers to questions would be. It became a game. Instead of going to all of the so-called 'go-sees' with my portfolio, I went straight to the very best photographers and asked them how they would see me in their photographs. Why would I have dragged photographs of myself around with me?

Did you regard Veruschka as an art project at the time? You had been an art student in Hamburg beforehand – when you still used the name Vera.

Yes, I did study painting. People continue to call me 'Germany's First Top Model' to this day, and I suppose that's what I will be until the day I die. But in fact I was never a typical model; I was more of an anti-model. I was never interested in looking pretty. Instead I saw modelling as a possibility to communicate – and to show people something really great. One could say that I applied my artistic intuition to fashion, and I did the very opposite of what is usually expected of models: keeping one's mouth shut, putting on clothes and just corresponding to the look that's in demand at that moment.

At that time, you worked almost exclusively in photographs and hardly ever on the catwalk. And yet in 2010 you surprisingly took part in a fashion show – for the British designer Giles Deacon at London Fashion Week. How did that come about?

Somehow I'm still in the minds of fashion people. Sometimes I find it astonishing myself. Helmut Newton used to say, 'We all work for the garbage' – sooner or later, all fash-

Veruschka among the reeds, shot for *Vogue* by Franco Rubartelli (1966)

Veruschka as a model in the cult movie *Blow-up* (1966, director: Michelangelo Antonioni)

ion magazines end up in the trash. But Newton and I are exhibited on museum walls, and people still like to remember Veruschka. I'm not friends with Giles Deacon or anything. I didn't even know his clothes until the request came in. And I also told him that I wasn't taking part in his show because of him.

Why then?

Because of the animals. I wanted to use the attention to give a voice to those who can't speak for themselves. Animals are sentient creatures, after all, and yet we use them as though they were commodities. And so every time somebody in London thrust a microphone at me and asked me about my ostensible modelling comeback, I said: 'No comeback, this is about something else', and then I talked about the brutality with which the fashion industry makes use of animals, and that the fur business is in full swing once again. Of course none of the fashion people wanted to hear about that. But that was my only motivation for getting back on the catwalk.

Apart from that, what did you think of the Deacon show?

Well, the make-up wasn't great. And the lighting was brutal. Neon light from above – that's deadly! You asked at the beginning what beauty is; light is everything, it makes people beautiful, and it makes them ugly. If I were a designer having a show, I would always first ask the question: 'Who is doing the lighting?' Because the same dress can unfold its beauty in the right light, and look absolutely miserable in cold neon light.

By the late 1960s you had begun to distance yourself from fashion and magazine photography, and since then you have primarily made portraits of yourself. In the photograph Wall Street Spider, *which was created in collaboration with the photographer Andreas Hubertus Ilse, you look like a spider crawling along a completely deserted Wall Street ...*

Andreas Hubertus Ilse and I took that photograph on a Sunday morning in the 1990s. We assumed that that would be the time when Wall Street would be at its emptiest. And indeed: when we arrived, the entire street had been sealed off, not a soul in sight, everything was spick and span – as though somebody had vacuumed the street. A Japanese television advert was about to be filmed there. So we asked whether we could take a photograph quickly before they started. That's how the picture came about. How lucky! And the photograph has also developed a completely different meaning as a result of the financial crisis, which didn't exist yet in the 1990s.

You became a spider, and in other photographs from the 1970s and 1980s you transformed yourself through body painting into plants and stones. Would it be correct to say that mimicry is your life's theme?

It would be. Even in the 1960s, when I did my shoots for *Vogue*, it was never just Veruschka on the photographs. Leaving aside the fact that Veruschka was herself an artificial figure, I tried in each of these situations to transform myself into another person. I didn't get in front of the camera to be the same person each time, but precisely in order to become somebody – or something – else. I was inspired by Marilyn Monroe, or by Brigitte Bardot, or by the way that Ursula Andress as a Bond Girl emerges from the sea. Later, animals and plants became further sources of inspiration, or – in an intense exploration of body painting together with the photographer Holger Trülzsch – the fascination of disappearing into the background entirely as a stone.

Susan Sontag wrote in 1986 in an essay about your body-painting portraits Transfigurations *that Veruschka was on the run from her own beauty ...*

Well, I suppose that was Susan Sontag's interpretation. I wouldn't say that I was on the run from my beauty. But perhaps it's true that I was looking for an escape so that I wouldn't always be trapped inside myself. In this context, I can't help thinking of my mother, who was a very beautiful woman. Throughout my life, I have often heard people who knew my mother say: 'Vera may be quite pretty – but her mother was a real beauty!'

Surely you have been asked whether you would like to be a judge in one of the model-casting shows on television?

I have indeed been approached on three occasions. I hope that, after the third rejection,

'Today you hear people at fashion shoots say: "No problem – we can adjust the head later." Why then should the model make an effort in front of the camera?'

the television channels have finally understood that I'm not available for that sort of thing.

Why not? Your colleague Twiggy has been a judge on *America's Next Top Model*, and the presenter of the show, Tyra Banks, likes to tell the young contestants about Veruschka …

No, I find these model-casting shows dreadful. Of course I could give the girls lots of advice; more than anything, I would encourage them to forget immediately everything they are taught on the show. Instead, they should do the very opposite. The problem with these shows is that the standard is emphasized more than what the models themselves have to offer. All individuality is exorcized from the girls. Apart from that, they always have to be made to cry. It's completely unnecessary.

What would you do differently in these shows?

First of all, I'd say to the girls: see it as a business, and keep your eyes on the money. Because as a model you are out of the business again in no time. Your career is over by the time you are in your early 20s, which is when my career had only just begun! And I would do away with all the bullying. I wouldn't teach the girls how they should walk, but would initially just let them walk the way they think looks good. And I would ask them which part of their face they think is strong – and then work out how that strength can be emphasized further. That's because I feel that the young models of today are almost indistinguishable from one another. Obviously I can still recognize Kate Moss, and one or two of the current German models, but all the rest have actually become very stereotypical. Of course that's also connected to the fact that photographs are increasingly heavily retouched. I wonder: since the faces are all reworked anyway, why don't they just use a digital prototype?

Do you mean that the model of the future will not step in front of a camera anymore?

Things seem to be moving in that direction. I imagine that at some point clients will go to modelling agencies and pay for the rights to use the appearance of a particular model, changing it according to their specifications. The models themselves will not have to show up at the fashion shoots anymore, as they will already have signed over a repertoire of typical poses and movements as digital images that are then assembled directly using Photoshop. If personality is no longer in demand anyway, that would be much more convenient for the model. It's already the case today that you hear people at fashion shoots say: 'No problem – we can adjust the head later.' Why then should you make an effort in front of the camera?

Veruschka in a denim jacket, 1970

Raf SIMONS

FASHION DESIGNER
Antwerp & Paris

For the past 20 years, Raf Simons has enjoyed one of the most unusual careers in the fashion world. After completing an internship with Walter Van Beirendonck, Simons – who studied industrial design in the late 1980s and early 1990s – realized that he would rather design fashion than furniture. His menswear label, launched in 1995, gained attention for its adaptations of styles from youth subcultures. In his shows, the Belgian designer, born in Neerpelt in 1968, featured post-punk music and – more frequently – techno. While serving as creative director for Jil Sander from 2005 to 2012, he designed his first, highly acclaimed collections for women. He was then recruited as John Galliano's successor at Dior, where – at his first prêt-a-porter show there – techno was once again the order of the day. This interview was conducted in Antwerp in 2010.

Mr. Simons, since the launch of your own brand and the debut of your men's collection in 1995 there have repeatedly been references to electronic music in your work, especially techno.

Yes, I love techno. I used to be a real club kid before I became a fashion designer at the age of 27. Clubbing and dancing were very important for me when I was a student. Actually it all started with the Belgian band Front 242. I went to see one of their concerts when I was 15. They played electronic body music and I thought they were totally amazing! As a teenager I also listened obsessively to Kraftwerk and electronic new wave records, Yazoo for example. Nowadays I hardly go dancing in clubs anymore, but I still have tremendous respect for techno producers. Richie Hawtin to begin with. I love his tracks! Since he debuted his Plastikman project in 1993, I play his music every day. I can't imagine life without Plastikman.

What exactly do you like about techno music?

Techno cannot be compared to classical music, of course, but what I like about good techno is that it is also really about composition. It is all about a beautiful build-up and a very elaborate layering of certain noises and sounds. The melodies might not be very important, techno can be quite minimal. Often it is about abstraction, which I like.

Your colleague Helmut Lang once said that techno created the last new silhouette in fashion. Would you agree?

Helmut Lang is one of my biggest heroes. Had it not been for him and for Martin Margiela – my other über-hero – I probably never would have started designing fashion. They were the ones who inspired me to do what I'm doing today. But to be honest, I don't see what Helmut means by that. I have never connected a specific silhouette to techno and I have never seen a style of dressing that was exclusively linked to this music. Can you think of one?

Maybe logos of record labels printed on T-shirts worn with camouflage cargo pants?

Well, you can go to a techno rave dressed like that, but there will be other people who look very different. Some will maybe wear a latex fetish outfit and others will wear a fake fur sweater. There was never one particular techno hairstyle either: long hair, short hair, shaved heads … Techno never had compulsory visual codes, ravers' outfits were very eclectic and drawn from totally different contexts. Within other genres of music, new wave and punk for example, that was totally different. These genres had their own very distinct dress codes. In the 1970s, when punk came about, nobody had ever, not in their whole lives, seen something that looked vaguely like punk!

When was the last time you saw a dress code that was linked to one distinct genre of electronic music?

For me, the last club music genre that had its very own style was new beat. Musically it was something in between EBM und acid. New beat never became very popular internationally after starting out as a strictly Belgian thing, a hardcore underground thing. It had a very short life-span. When new beat came about in 1988, it was completely new and created such a buzz that it became commercialized super-fast – after only one and a half years Belgian record companies started ripping off the style and released really tacky new beat cover versions of Belgian schlager hits. The original new beat club was the legendary Boccaccio in Ghent. I went there when I was 17 or 18. People there looked so extreme!

You, too? What were you wearing?

Black spandex biker shorts. All the new beat kids wore them. Also Dr. Martens shoes, the very heavy ones with round steel caps. We always cut the leather off the caps, so you could see the metal. Afterwards, when new beat had gone mainstream, you could buy shoes like this in the shops – but only the self-made ones were the real ones, of course. We also wore all kinds of colourful socks. The real fashion kids, if they could afford them, bought theirs from Tokio Kumagaï, a Japanese shoe designer who made socks in all rainbow colours, in checks and that kind of stuff. And everybody was wearing bomber jackets. There was no difference between men and women, everybody dressed totally alike, all of the men – straight or gay – looked super fashionable. There was also an influence from high fashion labels, for instance Jean Paul Gaultier or early Walter Van Beirendonck. Gaultier even released a new beat-related record …

You mean Gaultier's single 'How to Do That' from 1988?

Right, he produced that with Tony Mansfield, a British producer. So there was really an interesting overlap between club wear and the high fashion scene. The new beat hairstyles were also quite extreme: people were wearing massive, high backcombed quiffs, bleached or dyed black, or white and black together. And what I always found remarkable: everybody looked like that! If you went to the club, it was not that only a small, cool part of the crowd dressed like that. Everybody did.

That means you would have to dress up like that in order to be allowed into the club?

Not at all. People dressed like that all the time, not only at night. New beat was a whole lifestyle, you lived that life all the way, on the street, at daytime, even at work. Of course new beat also had its own dance style: you kind of stood still but moved your arms in a very expressive way. Maybe some of the arm movements had some connection to vogueing, but they looked much more robotic than that. And I'll also never forget:

Stills from a video for Raf Simons' spring/summer 2000 collection *Summa Cum Laude*

the Mercedes stars. Everybody was wearing them around their necks. I was getting my driver's license at the time and my dad had a friend who was dealing in old Mercedes cars. The stars got stolen from the hoods of his cars all the time, so he eventually gave up replacing them.

If new beat was the last distinct techno dress code, why haven't there been new ones after that?

That's a very difficult question. One of the reasons might be that, beginning in the 1990s, people within techno culture seemed to feel a certain ambiguity towards fashion and also performance. It felt like they preferred not to draw too much attention visually. So one could say that it has become increasingly difficult to come up with new dress codes. I also have the impression that young people – I hope I'm not sounding old here – are not so keen on developing their own specific style anymore. Instead of wanting to look different no matter what and maybe run the risk of looking ridiculous, they seem to prefer to be part of the aesthetic mainstream. And the ones who want to have their own look go for established subcultural dress codes of the past. That's why you still see punks, hippies, especially goths on the streets. Somehow these styles are still identified as 'different' – although they haven't changed over the last decades.

You did an internship at your colleague Walter Van Beirendonck's company in the early 1990s, before you started your own label. Were you involved in the development of his techno wear collection W.&L.T. which launched in 1993?

No, when Walter started W.&L.T. I had already left. My internship with him was around

Left: look from Raf Simons' spring/summer 2013 collection; right: look from Raf Simons' autumn/winter 2011/12 collection

1989 and 1990, after that I went back to the academy in Genk to finish my studies as an industrial designer. But even later, in the early 90s, I would sometimes still help Walter out with his presentations and shows in Paris.

Being a student of industrial design, why did you apply for an internship with a fashion designer?

I wasn't necessarily interested in fashion design back then, much more in furniture design, but I wanted to learn about the fashion environment. There was a lot of talk about the 'Antwerp Six' around that time, six graduates from the Fashion Department of Antwerp's Academy of Fine Arts. They were becoming known internationally. That was attracting me, I guess because there was not much else happening in Belgium – not in terms of creative approaches to design at least. Dries Van Noten and Ann Demeulemeester belonged to the 'Antwerp Six', and also Walter. He accepted my application although I was not a fashion student. I had faked a whole presentation map with drawings of excercises from an imaginary fashion school, using covers from *i-D*, *The Face* and so on. But Walter was not interested in all that. He liked the industrial design work that I had hidden in the back of my map. So during my internship he wanted me to design objects for his presentations – masks, for example, or fake perfume bottles. Walter always needed graphics, furniture and other stuff for his installations, because he never wanted to just design clothes, he always wanted to create total environments.

So during that time you decided to become a fashion designer?

I took that decision when Walter took me to Paris, where I saw my first real fashion show, during my internship, in 1989. It was Martin Margiela's third show. That evening I really connected with fashion. It was the first time that I saw how fashion could be conceptual, social, psychological, emotional – in other words: that fashion could be a very beautiful language. So I said to myself: that's what I'm going to do. But I didn't tell anyone yet. I still graduated as an industrial designer and it took me a few years to really start designing clothes.

You were speaking earlier about the ambiguity towards fashion and performance within techno culture ...

Well, when it comes to fashion, techno works very differently from rock. You can observe that not only in ravers and clubbers, but also in techno producers. It's complicated: techno is often produced by people who are not performers in the way people in rock bands are. And they don't want to be! They produce their music alone in their studio and at home. So visualization and performance can be bit of a challenge ...

But Kraftwerk gave the perfect blueprint for that already in the 1970s.

Exactly. Kraftwerk is the ultimate example that it can work. Their concept was waterproof right from the start, musically as well as visually. Kraftwerk practically appeared out of the blue, standing there like four robots dressed in black shirts, looking like they came from a monastery from the 1950s. They managed to create a perfect synthesis of music, stage performance and clothing. The single parts never distracted from each other – instead they amplified each other. Today you cannot see an image of Kraftwerk without instantly hearing their music in your head. Only very few people have succeeded in creating something similar since then – Green Velvet, Daft Punk and Aphex Twin being the exceptions. They have very convincing visualizations for their music as well, most of the time.

Looks from Raf Simons'
autumn/winter 2011/12
collection

Looks from Raf Simons' spring/summer 2011 collection

Daft Punk and Aphex Twin are also examples of techno artists who never – or at least very rarely – allow to be photographed. They prefer to hide their faces and disappear behind a well designed logo.

Obviously I'm not a musician, I'm a fashion designer, but I can connect to that in some way. I didn't want to be photographed myself for a while. I do not like to pose, I tend to be uncomfortable in front of cameras, and I think that my face and how I look is not necessarily connected to what I do as a designer. Who knows, maybe Daft Punk and Aphex Twin feel similar in relation to their work? Their music is not at all about their own faces, and yet they are aware that sound needs a strong visual image in order to be remembered. Aphex Twin's logo is especially strong in that respect. Maybe I would never have been interested in his music if I had not seen his logo in a techno store. Actually one of my best friends, Raymond Jacquemyns, designed the logo for the Belgian label R&S Records, on which Aphex Twin released some of his earliest records.

Within electronic music the format of the remix has always been very important. Does this concept also correlate to designing fashion?

It's not a word we use in fashion, but I understand and I like remixes. In fashion, lots of people actually do the act of remixing, but often it is not a conscious decision. It happens automatically. When you do things for a long time, it's in your genes to do them the way you do them. So no matter what you're designing, be it slim pants, or big pants, an oversized coat or a transparent shirt, it goes through your system and in

'My general drive is the psychology of the mirror, in a way. The whole idea of the individual performing towards his own image and performing towards other people.'

Looks from Raf Simons' spring/summer 2013 collection

this way it is linked to your aesthetic. But when I do something like a remix, I always say it. I never hide the information I use in my collections, I talk about references openly.

Especially your collaborations with brands like Dr. Martens or Fred Perry could be seen in this context. You take their iconic product and add your own twist.

You could indeed describe it as a remix – or maybe a remaster? When I collaborate with brands like Dr. Martens or Fred Perry, my interest is that they connect with so many different youth styles at the same time. I find that really fascinating, this whole social behaviour that their products are part of – pride, performance, attitude. In the 1980s for example, Dr. Martens shoes were not only worn by the new beat kids in Belgium, they were also popular in totally different scenes. In France, for instance, they were worn in a much more preppy environment. Not the big Dr. Martens with the steel toe, but the sharper ones. Still you wonder why different groups, each of them priding themselves on being individual, go for the same brand. What is it that they see in it?

That is basically a psychological question.

Right. I guess you could say that my general drive is the psychology of the mirror, in a way. The whole idea of the individual performing towards his own image and performing towards other people. I find this question eternally fascinating: how will another person perceive me and how do I want to perform towards another person? This is the main drive of my work, but I guess it's the drive of a lot of people who produce garments.

Michel GAUBERT

FASHION SHOW DJ

Paris

Although many fashion designers are themselves musically inclined, they prefer to trust Michel Gaubert's judgement when it comes to selecting soundtracks for their shows. From classical to abstract soundscapes to hip-hop, Gaubert provides the musical atmospheres for Chanel, Rodarte, Gucci, Céline, Moncler, Raf Simons, Balenciaga and a number of other labels. Through his behind-the-scenes work, Gaubert, a confidant of Karl Lagerfeld, has become so well known in his own right that Colette, the hip Paris luxury department store, now sells his CD compilations. In 2007, Longchamp even marketed an original Michel Gaubert collection with a DJ trolley case and other DJ accessories. This interview was conducted in 2011.

Monsieur Gaubert, in what way does music correspond with fashion?

Fashion and music are highly complementary. There are hardly any musicians who don't highlight their statements by dressing a certain way. Just think of Patti Smith, Kurt Cobain or Bryan Ferry. As soon as you hear their names, their music plays in your head and a specific look comes to mind. David Bowie, Prince, Michael Jackson. Music and fashion always work hand in hand.

Or to put it differently: if musicians use fashion for their art, why shouldn't fashion use music, too?

Of course. Fashion designers are often inspired by music, it brings images and ideas to their mind. Music can be important when a collection is designed, and it's important later, too, when the collection is presented.

Your friend Karl Lagerfeld recently debuted as a pop vocalist. In Rondo Parisiano, *a song produced by French duo SomethingALaMode, he says: 'Fashion and music are identical. Like fashion, music is a sign of its times. What would we think of the Baroque period if there had been no Baroque music?'*

Exactly. The Baroque period was a whole universe. Architecture, art, theatre, fashion and music – everything was linked. Looking back from the 21st century, it all makes sense. I guess it's not so easy to see how different fields relate to each other today – not everyone gets what a Jil Sander collection might have to do with Lara Croft. But it's not necessary to have centuries of historical distance, a few decades will do. For example, if you see *The Iron Lady*, the Margaret Thatcher film with Meryl Streep, you instantly think of new wave and punk music. The film shows the style of the late 1970s and early 1980s, and punk and new wave were the soundtrack of that period. There's one thing you have to keep in mind though when comparing the Baroque period with the 1980s or today: music is everywhere today, on the radio, on television, in restaurants, at the gym, in taxis, on aeroplanes. During the Baroque period, music was not part of everyday life, people heard it only in church, or maybe if they had access to the royal court. And in the 1980s, the era of MTV was just starting; there were no iPods yet. So actually, today there is too much music all the time. I think music is overused.

So if a fashion designer wants you to mix music for his show, you'd think of proposing to have silence instead?

Well, it would be a statement to have complete silence at a fashion show, definitely. To play no music at all would probably draw even more attentation than having a soundtrack. Up until now I never thought that was necessary. But of course I'd propose it if I had the feeling that it was the thing to do.

And you'd still get your fee?

Why not? The silence would be the outcome of my work as a sound advisor, wouldn't it?

Since when has music been a part of fashion shows?

Nobody seems to remember exactly. Legend has it that it was either Paco Rabanne or André Courrèges who started playing music in the 1960s. If you went to Chanel, Dior or Yves Saint Laurent at the time, there was no music. Fashion shows were completely different anyway. There was hardly any prêt-à-porter, only haute couture, photographers and camera teams were refused entry, and the shows dragged on forever – for hours! Today, they're only 15 minutes long.

What exactly did you mean earlier when you mentioned Jil Sander and Lara Croft?

I was talking about the winter collection Raf Simons designed for Jil Sander in 2010. Lara Croft was a big inspiration for it – you know, her fighting spirit, her power and looks. I've often worked on music with Raf. For the show, we took Lara Croft movies and extracted audio from different scenes, and then we rearranged the samples on the computer. It was quite a nightmare to do, but the outcome was great. There was no talking, only sounds, noises and atmospheres. The whole thing sounded quite abstract, a bit like the score from a Godard movie.

How does such a fashion mix work legally? Did you license the Lara Croft samples?

Of course not. If you use sound for a fashion show once, it's kind of a private thing, you don't worry about licensing. It's more difficult when the mix is being broadcast online

Michel Gaubert and his cat at home in Paris

'Karl said he had something very specific in mind, something with waltz and hip-hop. He asked me if I could make a mix for him and I said: "Sure."'

or on television. That's why in a lot of cases the videos of fashion shows you see on the internet don't really reflect what was going on musically, because certain parts of the audio have been replaced for copyright reasons. For example, if you look at the official video of the Chanel prêt-à-porter show from March 2011, all you hear are the parts of the soundtrack that I produced for the show. I had a string orchestra play variations of The Cure's song 'A Forest' in a studio. What you don't hear is that we actually mixed these new recordings with the original song and Robert Smith's original vocals.

Books in Michel Gaubert's apartment

An almost all-black collection, a set resembling an apocalyptic, charred forest and Robert Smith singing: 'I'm lost in a forest, all alone' – isn't this a bit too literal, too obvious?

Almost. There are no rules. Sometimes it can be wrong to play music that's so obvious, but sometimes it's perfect. One time there was a Chanel show – the prêt-à-porter spring/summer 2010 – for which Karl Lagerfeld had arranged a whole replica of the Maison Chanel to be set up in the Grand Palais in Paris. The runway was modelled after the street in front of the Maison, you know, Rue Cambon. So we decided to have the Madness song as the opening song: 'Our house, in the middle of our street.' That was very literal, of course, but it was also a funny surprise. The audience laughed, which made for a relaxed atmosphere right away.

How did your collaboration with Karl Lagerfeld start?

That was in 1990. I was working in a record store at the time. One day Karl came in, he was looking for new music. He said he had something very specific in mind for a fashion show, something with waltz and hip-hop. He asked me if I could make a mix for him and I said: 'Sure.'

He could have asked Malcolm McLaren, too. He would have been far more famous than you.

Well, yes, he could have. It was the time of McLaren's album *Waltz Darling*, which was all about a combination of waltz and hip-hop. But Karl asked me.

It's not easy to imagine him as a costumer going shopping for records.

But he often does it if he has the time. Karl loves record shopping! He still buys a lot of music.

So he hasn't transferred his musical expertise to you entirely? That's been the impression in recent years – that Karl Lagerfeld relies blindly on the fully loaded iPods that Michel Gaubert brings him.

It's true, I do bring him fully loaded iPods with new music. But he has his own iPods, too, on which he puts music that he buys online. Sometimes there are records that I wouldn't maybe listen to. I mean we all have our own taste.

How do your tastes differ?

Well, one of Karl's favourite composers is Stravinsky. He could listen to Stravinsky for hours. Maybe I can do it only for 25 minutes, you know. And I like dubstep. Maybe I would listen to a whole dubstep album and Karl would only find it interesting for five minutes, and then it would drive him crazy.

Had you worked as a fashion show DJ before Lagerfeld first asked you to work for him in 1990?

Yes. In the early 80s I was a DJ at a club in Paris. I met a few people there who asked me whether I would do music for their show. I tried it and it was fine. After that I got asked more and more, so that's how I became part of the game.

In which club were you a DJ?

At the Palace. That was basically the Parisian equivalent to New York's Studio 54 – the first club in town where all kinds of people would mix, straight people, gays, rock stars, the fashion scene and, you know, bad kids. I became a DJ there in 1979, one year after the club had opened. I played the basement called Le Privilège, which was supposed to be something like a chill-out room – before it was called that. Punk, jazz, new wave, I played everything. Fridays and Saturdays. Quite a legendary place.

The British fashion journalist Alicia Drake writes about Le Palace in her book *The Beautiful Fall*. Celebrities allegedly shot heroin downstairs in the séparée.

Yes, it was all pretty hardcore. Coke, heroin, sex. People did everything out in the open back then, they didn't mind if someone was watching. Me neither.

In *The Beautiful Fall,* the club is also described as the place where Karl Lagerfeld and Yves Saint Laurent – and their respective entourages – battled out their rivalry.

Well, I don't know if it really happened that way; Alicia Drake is probably exaggerating. Of course, you had all kinds of fashion people in the club. They can be bitchy some- times. Thierry Mugler was a regular, the staff of Le Palace was dressed by him. Claude Montana was hanging out there all the time. Twice a year the club had big fashion balls, so Karl and Saint Laurent would come with their whole entourages. Issey Miyake and Kenzo came, too. Kenzo was friends with both Karl and Saint Laurent. I never witnessed any open rivalry.

Did you know Karl Lagerfeld at the time?

Only by sight. We never talked at the Palace. We got to know each other only later, when he came up to me at the record store.

Do you remember whether he was a good dancer at the Palace?

I must have seen him dance often, but I don't remember watching him. I realized only later that he's a great dancer. He's very good at mambo, for example.

Mambo?

Yes, Karl loves the mambo! He also likes the cha-cha-cha. He's very into Afro-Cuban dances, and he's also passionate about the waltz. He even took proper dancing classes!

Coming back to the fashion shows: how important is it to always play the latest tracks?

Not important at all. Playing the latest trendy and unreleased music doesn't mean anything anymore. Everyone does it. You know, I said earlier that music is everywhere today – that also means it's very accessible. It's almost impossible to stay one step ahead with music anymore. We start with New York Fashion Week in September, and then when you go to Paris Fashion Week in October all the good new music has been played already. You've heard everything. So I sit down with the designers and we think about what else we can come up with.

So one strategy to avoid *future fatigue* is to delve deeper into the archives and surprise the audience with older music?

In a way, yes. Classical music has in fact become more important in recent years. Even at Raf Simons. When Raf needed music for his autumn/winter 2011 Jil Sander show, we took orchestra parts from the score of Hitchcock's *Spellbound* and mixed them with some techy sounds and a little bit of hip-hop. And when Nicolas Ghesquière had some kind of punk collection at Balenciaga, he wanted to play hardcore music, but then we decided it would be too obvious – so we ended up using Handel's aria 'Lascia ch'io pianga'. Lars von Trier used it in his film *Antichrist*. Classical music can be very cinematic, you know, it evokes big emotions. And fashion is all about big emotions!

Michel Gaubert enjoying a smoke, 2011

Once you even hired a full-size symphony orchestra for a Chanel show.

Yes, 80 musicians played live at the Grand Palais for the spring/summer 2011 haute couture show. The inspiration for the collection was Alain Resnais's film *Last Year at Marienbad*.

For which Coco Chanel designed costumes in 1961.

Exactly. I couldn't use the film's original score for the show, though. Cinematically, *Last Year at Marienbad* might be one of the most beautiful films ever made, but its score is quite schizophrenic and obsessive. It was composed by Francis Seyrig, the brother of the main actress, Delphine Seyrig – who wears Chanel in the film. The score is really strenuous, a lot of atonal harpsichord sounds. At a fashion show it would have driven people mad. Karl wanted a light atmosphere, to make the whole show feel like a stroll in the park.

So you had the orchestra play pop songs, by Björk, for example.

Yes. Karl wanted an orchestra, but not classical music. So I thought of using pop songs and did some research on pop music that uses orchestra. 'Isobel' and 'Bachelorette', the Björk songs, came up quickly. Their orchestration is beautiful, not too classical, but not too pop either. Perfect for the show!

Malcolm MCLAREN

FASHION SITUATIONIST
New York

Although he never called himself a fashion designer, over the past 40 years Malcolm McLaren has left an indelible imprint on the field – both alone and in collaboration with Vivienne Westwood. Born in London in 1946, the young, hippie-hating, Guy Debord-reading art student McLaren invented a new form of provocation – 'fashionable Situationism'. His leather fetish articles and T-shirts in that style first went on sale on London's King's Road in the 1970s. McLaren went on to found and manage the Sex Pistols, and later promoted and profited from recent American subcultural exports like hip-hop and vogueing. This interview was conducted in late 2009, just a few months before McLaren's unexpected death in April 2010.

Mr. McLaren, so it all started with Elvis Presley's electric-blue lamé suit?

Exactly. That was in 1971. I'd just been expelled from art school and was looking for a fight. So I copied the blue lamé suit I'd seen on a photo of Elvis, put it on and went strutting up and down King's Road. I thought: who knows, maybe I'll be discovered! But no one so much as batted an eyelid. It was embarrassing. So as I was just about to take refuge in the telephone box at the end of the road, this fellow came up to me and said: 'Hey, there's still some space in my shop, 430 King's Road, here's the key'. And there it was: I was the owner of a shop.

You called it Let It Rock, and the rest is history.

Yes, it's a great story! The owner disappeared and said we should look after his things – but he never came back. So I ran the shop together with Vivienne Westwood, the woman to whom I had lost my virginity in 1965 and who immediately got pregnant. At first I didn't want to have anything to do with the child. My grandmother gave me money for an abortion, but Vivienne took it to buy a cashmere twinset on Bond Street instead. Later on I did accept the baby. Today, I'm actually very proud of my son.

His name is Joseph Corré and his Agent Provocateur label sells exclusive lingerie very successfully.

In some respects, Joseph is carrying on the family tradition. Apart from the fact that his mother is a world-famous designer, his grandfather was also a master tailor. And my stepfather owned a chain of clothing stores. I myself have never really seen myself as a fashion designer – even though Vivienne and I designed clothes together. From the very start I always saw myself more as an artist. For example, part of my art concept was to keep on closing down our shop. As soon as business was thriving we would close and reopen with a different name and a different concept. After Let It Rock the shop was called Too Fast to Live, Too Young to Die, then Sex, then Seditionaries, and finally World's End. The potential of spectacular failures!

Is that what you understood by the term 'fashionable Situationism'?

Yes, it was a form of protest. That's what Situationism was about. I'd never heard of the Situationist International, until the student riots broke out in Paris in 1968. The only hint of revolt that my generation had dared to go public with previously were the copies of Thomas de Quincey's *Confessions of an English Opium-Eater* or William Burroughs' *Naked Lunch* that kept hanging out of our trouser pockets. Situationism finally brought a bit of action. At the centre of it all was the demand that there be no distinction between life and art. It was similar in some ways to the Fluxus movement a few years earlier – even though the Fluxus crowd was of course much more esoterically inclined than we were.

One of the most famous Fluxus artists today is Yoko Ono.

I've never met her. But I did meet John Lennon. That was a strange story – do you want to hear it?

But of course!

That was in the 1970s, in New York. I went to a club, wearing a fantastic suit that I'd made for myself. John Lennon was there, too, without Yoko, but with a few other men. Suddenly one of his companions came up to me and said that John Lennon thought my suit was great. I said I was happy to hear it, because I'd made it myself. Then the man said that John Lennon would like to have the suit. I said that unfortunately it wasn't for sale; it was the only one of its kind. So the man said I hadn't understood what he was saying: Mr. Lennon wanted the suit right away. And the way he said it made it clear that it wouldn't be a good idea to refuse John Lennon's request. I couldn't believe my ears!

And John Lennon?

He kept on looking in the opposite direction. The man said I should hand over my suit immediately, and he would have someone fetch me some new clothes from my hotel room. I was suddenly frightened. So I went to the restroom with him and spent the next hour standing in my underpants in one of the cubicles, freezing to death – until the fellow brought me something new to wear. John Lennon, of course, had long disappeared. What a nightmare!

Let's get back to fashionable Situationism.

Well, the Situationist International had these great slogans: 'It is forbidden to forbid', 'Be realistic, demand the impossible', and so on. At the end of the 1960s, these slogans gave people like me, who had just left art school, carte blanche. I abandoned the ideal of objective beauty as the classical vision of art. I wanted to turn art into something quite different. Becoming the manager of a clothes shop and the manager of an ersatz pop band called Sex Pistols allowed me to do just that. With those little sex hooligans I staged cultural terror attacks for the benefit of our planet!

One could also say that with the Sex Pistols you successfully stylized an attitude of refusal into a commercial spectacle – while Guy Debord, the mastermind behind Situationism, emphasized his rejection of the spectacle of capitalism.

That's right. The things we did were not exactly what Debord had in mind. But in 1977, when the Sex Pistols were No. 1 in the charts in England with 'God Save the Queen', I got a phone call. It was Guy Debord, and he said: 'Thank you for making my record such a big hit.' At first I didn't understand what he meant. But that's really how he saw it: 'God Save the Queen' was *his* No. 1. It was his idea. The success of the Sex Pistols was due to Situationist tactics such as *détournement* and guerilla communications.

The punk clothes that you designed with Vivienne Westwood are still much sought-after today. Is it true that in 2008 Damien Hirst paid 80,000 pounds at Sotheby's for some clothes that, it was claimed, came from Sex and Seditionaries, but were actually fakes?

Yes, it's unbelievable! Scotland Yard's files contained 3,500 pages of evidence. It was a huge affair. It turned out that there was a whole factory in London producing the fakes. At this factory, fashion students from Central Saint Martins College of Art and Design made copies of our old collections for a shady businessman – 'No Future' jackets, 'Destroy' waistcoats, 'Karl Marx' T-shirts, bondage trousers, all sorts of trashy tops with swastikas on them and so on. And 25 museums from all over the world, including the Metropolitan Museum of Art in New York and the Victoria & Albert Museum in London, had bought the clothes at auctions and shown them in exhibitions. Vivienne didn't want to have anything to do with it, but I went to Scotland Yard myself, examined the clothes and officially declared them to be fakes.

'And then all this junk is seen hanging in museums all over the world, with my name on it!'

At Let It Rock in 1972: McLaren holding a Teddy Boy outfit designed by himself and Vivienne Westwood.

Bondage suit by Malcolm McLaren und Vivienne Westwood, 1976

Wouldn't it have been more amusing and above all more Situationist, if you had said: 'No, they're all genuine?'

Of course. But you can't imagine how badly made these items were. They were stitched together from completely different fabrics, the label was different, the seams were in the wrong places, and so on. I'm not going to honour a poor copy by saying: 'Yes, I made that.' And then all this junk is seen hanging in museums all over the world, with my name on it! I really felt sorry for my good friend Damien Hirst, who showed me all his plastic bags filled with the rubbish he'd bought. But I think that's the point: people want more than anything to believe that something is genuine.

You say that you have never seen yourself as a fashion designer. Nonetheless, in 2009, you designed a collection for the exclusive skatewear label Supreme from New York.

Not really. I didn't design the collection – I *endorsed* it. I allowed Supreme to use my name, and I supplied them with the artwork from my *Duck Rock* album. The people at Supreme used it as they liked, and they printed its motifs on their T-shirts, sweaters and trainers. Not only was it much easier for me, it was also much more satisfactory for Supreme. Because I really am a bit too old to know what skaters like – don't you think?

In principle, the collection could also be called a Keith Haring collection – after all, he was the one who created the artwork for your Duck Rock album.

Yes, Keith was incredible. He just couldn't keep still. He had to keep drawing all the time; he even sketched things on paper napkins. Graffiti was the big thing when I recorded *Duck Rock* in 1982, and Keith had his own inimitable style. Very tribalistic. It fitted my concept perfectly – because even if *Duck Rock* is still regarded primarily as a hip-hop album, it was really a world music concept album, in which I combined all sorts of Caribbean and African tribal and folk music with the sound of the Zulu nation.

The people at Supreme were actually more interested in Keith Haring than they were in you?

Well, they were very keen to produce something using the artwork from that album. And I must say I find what Supreme do with their label very interesting. Basically, they're only interested in a very specific period in New York, from the early to mid-1980s. Their entire aesthetic is based on that era. They're absolutely obsessed with this idea of authenticity.

And yet it's hard to imagine anything less authentic than Duck Rock, a hip-hop world music album by Malcolm McLaren, produced by the plastic pop maestro Trevor Horn.

You're probably right. But apart from the fact that it was Keith Haring who created the artwork for the album, *Duck Rock* was also authenticated in retrospect – when people from the hip-hop scene discovered the album and sampled it repeatedly, especially the song 'Buffalo Gals'.

So you mean that something becomes authentic if people like it and sample it?

Maybe!

Let's also speak about the musical you've supposedly been working on for years. It's said to be about Christian Dior.

That's correct. To be precise, I actually wanted to produce this musical back in the 1980s – when I worked in Hollywood supplying ideas for Columbia Pictures while I was Steven Spielberg's muse. The plan was that I would develop Broadway musicals for him. It was a frustrating period in my life. First my film project *Heavy Metal Surf Nazis* fell through, and then my idea of writing a waltz and square dance musical about the history of the United States failed. The research took too long; suddenly six months had passed and there were new projects – that's how this business works. But I never completely gave up the idea.

But why a musical about Dior?

I find his life story really fascinating. Dior played a major role in reviving the glamour of haute couture and re-establishing Paris as the world's centre of fashion after the Second World War. In my musical I want to concentrate on the decade from 1947 to 1957, from his first collection until his death. Dior was very musical; his favourite song was 'Que Sera, Sera'. And of course there was the perpetual rivalry between him and Coco Chanel. Chanel hated Dior – just as she hated all gay fashion designers, because she believed that gays should be banned from dressing women. After Chanel returned to Paris in 1954 from her exile in Switzerland, she was much more successful than Dior. And yet she had collaborated with the Nazis during the Occupation. She was the mistress of Baron Hans Günther von Dincklage, a special attaché of the Third Reich's Propaganda Ministry in France. These are all details that get left out of the film versions of Coco Chanel's life.

And what about Dior? Do you find him interesting also from a fashion point of view?

I do! Believe it or not, his famous first collection from 1947 paved the way for rock'n'roll. With this collection, Dior defined the so-called 'New Look', although it wasn't really new at all. Basically, Dior tried to make the costumes of his mother and the hourglass silhouette of the Belle Époque fashionable again. It's hard to imagine anything more bourgeois or reactionary. My grandmother, for example, the daughter of a wealthy family of Dutch-Portuguese diamond merchants, simply loved Dior. But a few years later, this look became an expression of non-conformity and rebellion in the United States, during the birth of teenage culture. What a paradox! The look had absolutely nothing to do with feminism, emancipation or other new developments; it laced women up in corsets again. And yet it became the defining silhouette of rapid change. Wasp waist, circle skirt, crinoline: that's what the rock'n'roll girls of the 1950s looked like.

You mean the girls in the James Dean film *Rebel Without a Cause*?

Exactly.

Didn't this film also include a very early punk statement? One of the main characters, Plato, wears different-coloured socks – a blue one and a red one.

I know. But in those days that wasn't a punk statement. The film's costume designer, Moss Mabry, was merely trying to point out how totally rattled poor Plato is. The film shows all too clearly that the boy is not only stark staring mad, but is also hopelessly in love with Jim Stark, the character played by James Dean. And what do you do when you're a complete mess? You don't really pay attention to what you're wearing. Maybe this detail provided inspiration for punks later on. In any case, it looked pretty good.

Malcolm McLaren at his home in London in 1983; suit and trainers from Vivienne Westwood's *Witches* collection, autumn/winter 1983/84

Walter Van BEIRENDONCK

'Kiss the Future!' was the advertising slogan of Walter Van Beirendonck's cyber-punk-technowear label W.&L.T., during the heyday of rave in the 1990s. To a large degree, the slogan still stands: Van Beirendonck's aesthetic is as full of colour and play as ever, and today his menswear is regarded just as extraordinary, or even daring. In the late 1970s, Van Beirendonck – who was born in Brecht, Belgium, in 1957 – was a classmate of Dries Van Noten, Ann Demeulemeester and Martin Margiela at the Royal Academy of Fine Arts in Antwerp. Later on, he co-founded the legendary 'Antwerp Six' designer group. As a teacher at the Royal Academy, he has since guided and influenced several generations of young Belgian and international fashion designers.

Well, I like the whole colour spectrum, especially bright and strong shades, which are a very important part of my language. The first thing I think about when I start a new collection is always colours, and colour moods – long before I think about fabrics or prints.

Do colours express something specific for you? Take red for example: what does it stand for in Walter Van Beirendonck's world?

I never use colour in a literal sense. Some colours have symbolic value, of course, they're related to certain meanings, but that's not what it's about for me. If I feel that I need to combine a bright fluo pink with a pastel, I just do it – because I think it's beautiful. Certain colours stay with me forever. One specific red for example, 'Flame Scarlet' – a very strong red with a touch of orange. Its name is from the Pantone colour chart. Actually, in my studio I speak almost a kind of Pantone language. If I say 'Blossom Pink', they all know: 'Ah, he's talking about Pantone 1767' – a very bright pink, almost rose.

The pieces from your collections that are motley-coloured probably don't sell as well as the more toned down, plain or pastel-coloured ones?

Quite the contrary. You could even say: the stronger, the better. Customers who come to me want colour. People who prefer something discreet or black, well, they can go to other designers – Rick Owens or Damir Doma for example. In any case, if I do something black – which happens from time to time – it's hardly sold. But of course, it can be difficult to be taken seriously if you dress very colourfully, at least in Western societies. I think that's very stupid, because actually it's a sign of strength if you wear a bright red suit or a bright orange suit instead of a black one. You're making a statement. People will look at you differently, and that's a powerful moment, because you're forcing them to position themselves in relation to you.

In the course of your career, which spans more than 30 years, has it ever happened that you saw a person wear one of your designs in public and you caught yourself thinking: 'Wow, this looks pretty odd?'

No. But I remember thinking 'Wow, this is odd' back in the 1990s when I went to a flea market in London and stumbled across a whole stall full of W.&L.T. copies. Quite shameless! You know, W.&L.T. was the street wear label I designed at the time for the German denim brand Mustang – the abbreviation stood for 'Wild and Lethal Trash'. Back then, we did T-shirts with all-over prints that were very popular: space prints, nature prints, and so on. Apparently our T-shirts were also very popular with the fakers! Actually, as a designer you might feel honoured when your designs are copied, but in this case the fakes were done so cheaply and they looked so bad that it really pissed me off.

For a while, with W.&L.T., you succeeded in translating the visual spirit of the rave and techno culture of the 1990s into fashion.

I was never a raver myself, though. I was sympathetic to the spirit of the techno movement and I also liked the music – but I would never have called myself a raver. I certainly didn't look like one. Sometimes people were irritated by that. One time for example – I think it was in Munich – there was a big rave and I wanted to go with some of my assistants. But the bouncers at the entrance told me: 'No, we won't let you in because you look like a hard rocker.' Which was absurd, because when I looked around at the queue there were hundreds of ravers dressed from head to toe in W.&L.T.!

W.&L.T.'s success lasted a few years, but by the early 2000s the label seemed to become more and more trashy. You had left already in 1999.

Yes, during the peak years, we had 600 shops worldwide and sales were going very well. But in the late 1990s the whole mood changed dramatically. First of all, the fashion world started to head more and more in a marketing direction, and fashion itself was getting more serious. You know, suddenly you had Prada Sport popping up, this whole black nylon thing – a very slick look. Obviously this was the complete opposite of what I was doing at W.&L.T. At that time, the Mustang people started to push me to change my signature. But I didn't want to do that, it felt very wrong to me. Originally, when I first met them, they'd been doing their boring jeans thing forever and they seemed kind of desperate, and they wanted me to help them move forward and reach a younger, louder audience. Now, suddenly, they wanted to become more boring again. So I broke my contract and started again from scratch on my own. I had to fire my

Looks from the autumn/winter 2013/14 collection *Shut Your Eyes to See*

*'I wouldn't say
I was a pioneer of
today's internet
aesthetic. Even before
Google arrived I had
established my own
system for
researching
inspirations.'*

Backstage at the *Shut Your Eyes to See* show
at the Théâtre du Châtelet in Paris in January 2013

whole team, more than 25 people. It was a huge decision, but it was the right thing to do.

You said in an interview that reading *Snow Crash,* Neal Stephenson's cyber punk novel from 1992, had been very influential on the whole W.&L.T. aesthetic.

Yes, this book actually changed my way of thinking. I was so fascinated by its whole story about avatars and digital life and digital identities. Neal Stephenson was very forward-thinking, but what was so gripping about the book was that the future that he described in it had actually already started by that time – in the early 1990s the internet was just beginning to make its impact, and communication was already changing. In fact several of my collections were inspired by *Snow Crash*, for example the *Avatar* collection from 1997. And W.&L.T. was also the first fashion label to have its own website.

Looking back at your collections from the 1980s – from the time before W.&L.T. – one gets the impression that you were already making use of Google back then in order to find images from disparate cultures and meld them together. Mexican wrestlers' masks, cartoon characters, Turkish folklore, S&M gear ...

You mean I was a pioneer of today's eclectic internet aesthetic? I wouldn't say that. Even before the internet and Google arrived I had established my own system for researching various inspirations in all possible ways, you know, through books, libraries, galleries, museums, magazines about art or ethnology. That's still my method today. I'm really fascinated by a lot of different things and I try to get as much input as possible, and then

Walter Van Beirendonck's retrospective *Dream the World Awake* at the ModeMuseum Antwerp, 2011

my head starts to translate all that input into a kind of Walter language. It's never about transferring something that has inspired me directly into an idea, or staying true to the original. But context is important. Actually, if I look at how my students at the Academy use the internet today, it's quite a different thing.

<u>Since 1983, you've been teaching fashion at the Royal Academy of Fine Arts in Antwerp, where you studied.</u>

Right. It's easy to just go to Google and stumble across a certain topic there. But I often have the impression that my students don't seem to be interested in going deeper to really learn about the whole thing. You know, it's quite superficial. They print out the image of an artwork that they say they find fascinating – but when I ask them who the artist is, they say: 'I don't know.' Unbelievable! I scold them: 'Context!' How can you understand an artwork if you don't even know the name of the artist, let alone know anything about the circumstances in which the work was created?

<u>How do you remember the time of the early 1980s when you were a student yourself and about to graduate?</u>

Well, when I left my small home village and came to study at the Academy in Antwerp in the 1970s, I was full of enthusiasm and especially inspired by the whole glam rock thing, you know, David Bowie and his *Ziggy Stardust* look. But then, after graduating, I became disillusioned quite quickly. Back then there was no fashion scene in Belgium, nobody seemed to care or take notice; also, there were no media, no magazines, nothing whatsoever! Plus there was the language barrier. I mean, who speaks Flemish? We were all eagerly reading English magazines like *The Face* and we were quite jealous of everything that happened in London – and at the same time we felt we were buried alive in Belgium.

<u>When you say 'we' you mean the 'Antwerp Six', a group that you formed with fellow students like Dries Van Noten and Ann Demeulemeester?</u>

Exactly. We were all graduates from the Royal Academy and very ambitious. We wanted to break free from our Belgian jail, so to speak. That's why we stuck together and went to London as a group in the mid-80s.

<u>In London, did people grant you some kind of outsider's bonus?</u>

Look from the autumn/winter 2011/12 collection *Hand on Heart*

Definitely. If one of us had gone to London on his own, he probably would have been ignored. But when we arrived there as a group, six Belgians all at once, it made us even more special. Apart form that, we were already quite professional at the time, you know, we had at least some maturity. Each one of us had already worked on his own collection in Belgium for a few years, so all the clothes were properly made, we knew how to present them and we also knew how to write a press release. I think that's why the English press decided to take us seriously. And maybe it made us even more special that we didn't have one consistent group aesthetic. In fact, our collections looked totally different.

Did you come up with that name, Antwerp Six, yourselves?

No, the fashion press in London invented that name because they couldn't pronounce our Flemish names. I guess they were too complicated for them.

To this day, a lot of people think that Martin Margiela was a member of the Antwerp Six – which is wrong, isn't it?

Yes. Actually, at the very beginning, Martin was part of our group. There were originally seven of us. He had studied with us at the Royal Academy in Antwerp for four years – he was in my class. But he didn't come with us to London. Martin decided instead to leave on his own for Paris, where he started to work for Gaultier.

When he was a fellow student, was he already this mystery man who shies away from the public and doesn't allow himself to be photographed?

No, not at all. That came later. Actually, Martin is quite a normal person with regular communicative skills and he gets along with everybody. There are no huge peculiarities or weird habits. He created this whole anonymity concept and the no-photo policy in order to get attention. It was a choice he made. I think it was related to the fact that he worked in Paris at Gaultier around a time when there was a real Gaultier hysteria, you know. In the mid-80s the media couldn't get enough of Gaultier, everybody wanted a piece of him and Gaultier staged himself accordingly. I think that's when Martin decided: I'll do the exact opposite. The mystery was a marketing idea. And it started to work very well for him.

Raf Simons launched his label in Antwerp about ten years after the advent of the Antwerp Six and he also refused to be photographed initially. Is it true that he was an intern at your label in the early 1990s?

Yes, but this is really not so special. Almost all of the Belgian fashion designers from the younger generation have studied with me or been interns at my label. The students who came to the Academy from abroad, too – Bernhard Willhelm for example. They've all worked at my studio.

But when Raf Simons was an intern with you, he hadn't decided on becoming a fashion designer yet. And he didn't study in Antwerp, he was training to be an industrial designer in Genk.

You're right. For his application, Raf had jotted down some fashion drawings, very quickly, but when I looked in the back of his portfolio, there were also product and furniture designs, which I found more interesting. So at the beginning, I didn't work with him so much on fashion, but he designed mainly things that were related more to presentation – booths for trade fairs for example. Raf enjoyed working at my studio

Sculptures from Walter Van Beirendonck's spring/summer 2013 collection *Cloud #9*, designed in collaboration with Austrian artist Erwin Wurm

a lot, and I guess you really could say that that was when he discovered his enthusiasm for fashion. Later on, he also worked on buttons and zippers and all those things for me. I also remember that I took him to Paris to see some of his first fashion shows, by Margiela for example.

Today, Raf Simons is famous – but you don't sound too proud.

Of course I'm proud! But I'm not one to praise myself, and I certainly won't start printing T-shirts with a slogan saying: 'I'm the one who turned Raf Simons on to fashion design.'

Instead, you like to print other slogans on T-shirts: 'Kiss the Future', 'Dream the World Awake', 'Don't worry, there is a happy ending'. What makes you such an optimistic sloganizer?

Since the very beginning of my career, I've never seen my work only as fashion design. For me it has always been about communication. I like to tell stories, and I do that through my collections. Working with language is an important part of that. So in a way, these slogans emphasize the feeling of positivity that my clothes should convey – you know, an optimism about the future and our search for a better world.

A future all-digital world in which we may not need clothing anymore?

Who knows! In any case, we'll always need fashion design. Avatars should look very good, too.

Diane PERNET

FASHION BLOGGER

Paris

Strange as it may sound, Diane Pernet is the grande dame of fashion blogging. When she launched her own blog, *A Shaded View on Fashion*, in 2005, she was one of the very first people in the field to make use of the then young online medium. Since then, Pernet has consistently focused her independent gaze on fashion, while making ventures into the neighbouring fields of design, film, art and music. Hardly any other blog features so many unknown but soon-to-be-famous names. In 2008, the American-born fashion expert added a fashion film festival of her own – *A Shaded View on Fashion Film* – to her many activities. The festival's home venue is the Centre Pompidou in Paris, but it has also made successful guest appearances in Milan, London and Antwerp. Before moving to Paris in 1990, Pernet worked as a fashion designer in New York.

Madame Pernet, for more than 30 years you have dedicated your life to fashion, but interestingly you never changed your own look. Why?

I am quite addicted to my look. Clothes should always make you feel good and be comfortable. While some people have a need to impress others by what they wear, personally, I just like to please myself. There was a line in David Cronenberg's film *Spider* that I found remarkable in this regard – it went something like this: 'The less there is of the man, the more he needs the clothes.' In the film, Ralph Fiennes plays the schizophrenic Dennis, who wears a number of different shirts layered on top of each other. I think there is really something to that observation.

You mean the more stable a character, the more unitary their wardrobe?

I wouldn't call it unitary. When I was younger I was experimenting with my look all the time, as others do, searching for whatever I felt was an outward expression of the real me. That was entertaining for a while. But at a certain point I found the look that really felt like me, and I suppose I just stayed with it. Maybe we call that style as opposed to fashion.

If everbody found their own style, the fashion industry would be finished in no time. Wouldn't it?

Interesting point, but then again, within one style you can always find new elements. My silhouette never changes and it is always black – but that doesn't mean that I am always wearing the same clothes.

In New York you worked as a designer for 13 years. What kind of clothes did you design?

My clothes were for strong and sensual women, and my collections weren't all black, if that's what you think. In fact I offered a lot of colours. I was interested in using many different textures, and I created certain new textiles with a manufacturer. Many people considered my clothes avant-garde at the time, but I did not think that they were difficult to wear. Let's say that I've always walked to my own beat, and while disco madness was going on I was quite minimal and streamlined. My clothes were often copied one season later and by then the market was more ready for them – but I was off to the next thing already.

The New York club scene of the late 70s and early 80s is legendary. Were you part of it?

Yes, completely. NYC in the 80s was really an exciting period and I liked to go out a lot. I remember the first time I saw Klaus Nomi perform with his band Strange Party, which included Joey Arias as a back-up singer. Keith Haring was throwing great parties at the Paradise Garage. I also often went to the Mudd Club, Danceteria, Save the Robots, The Michael Todd Room at the Palladium, Area, the Roxy … that was definitely my scene, much more than Studio 54. I did fashion shows at Xenon, Limelight and Bonds. The owners were always offering me their spaces for free, lights, invitations, etc. And I would give after-parties at their expense. I was kind of the Queen of Downtown!

Did you live in Downtown?

Yes, my first address was on 17th and Broadway, which was right across the street from Andy Warhol's Factory. And then I lived on Bleeker and 11th street in the West Village for 13 years, which is now across the street from the Marc Jacobs boutique …

Did you know Marc Jacobs at the time?

I met Marc in the early 80s when he was still a student at Parsons and I think, if my memory serves me well, that he was a dresser for one of my shows. I went to see his first show, in which he had all those smiley face sweaters that his grandmother had knitted for him. Marc was an instant success with the press. I am very happy for him.

The early 90s seem to be a turning point in your life. You abandoned design and left New York. What happened?

New York in the late 80s was a really rough and cruel place. Mental hospitals were turning out their patients, who became part of the huge army of the city's homeless. When they cleaned up Washington Square park, all the homeless crackheads from there moved across the street from me. I didn't feel comfortable leaving my house anymore. And a lot of my friends were dying of Aids. Klaus Nomi was the first friend to come down, and soon nearly the entire neighborhood was sick or dead. I had to leave because it was just too sad and heavy for me to stay there, let alone be creative.

In France, you started out working as a costume designer for film, right?

Yes, my first job was on the set of Amos Gitai's *Golem – l'esprit de l'exil*. The subject of the film was quite heavy obviously, but I had the opportunity to dress Hanna Schygulla. Having always been a big fan of Rainer Werner Fassbinder, that was a huge honour for me. I had seen every film of Fassbinder's that she had ever acted in! So for Amos Gitai I had to make her look like a spirit in the woods, and the night before the shoot Amos told her that he wanted her to be nude. She was around 50 at the time and this was not acceptable for her. So my job was to make her look nude and also keep her warm but not make her look fat. I remember I made her a body suit that I latex-painted on a stand-in for her. So when Hanna put on this suit, after hours and hours of waiting for the shoot to begin, she had to use the bathroom … I realized that I had completely forgotten about how she was going to be able to do that!

This should have been caught on film – you could have shown it at your festival A Shaded View on Fashion Film!

Well, in fact my experiences as a costume designer did play a big part in launching the film festival in 2008. Most film directors are afraid of fashion. They don't realize how fashion can really support a character, sometimes with the most subtle sort of detail. Strangely, French directors are the worst: they seem to love putting their actors in plaid shirts and rubber boots. But fashion can embrace film so nicely! Just think of Gena Rowland's sunglasses in John Cassavetes' *Opening Night*, or the great snakeskin jacket that Marlon Brando wears in *The Fugitive Kind*. Or think of the way Kenneth Anger made shiny flapper dresses dance on clothes hangers in his short film *Puce Moment* – it seems like they're moving right towards the camera in a dry cleaner's!

Is it these styling ideas that qualify a movie as a fashion film?

*'You know,
dead people who
come rising from
the bath tub or
people who take
out their eyes ...
this had such an
impact on me!'*

Diane Pernet's trademark look: black veil,
sunglasses, metal spider pins in her hair.
Paris, 2010

I get that question sometimes. I think any film where fashion is a protagonist in some way can be shown at a fashion film festival, no problem. I want it to be open. I don't consider a beautiful model in movement in front of a camera a fashion film! I also have to think of David Lynch and Peter Greenaway. They are directors who have always seen the value of fashion. Greenaway collaborated with Jean Paul Gaultier for *The Cook, the Thief, His Wife & Her Lover* ...

You seem to be a person who really thinks in filmic images ...

Yes, film has been my life since I was a little kid. My parents took me to see films like *Diabolique* and *Eyes Without a Face* when I was eight or nine. You know, dead people who come rising from the bath tub or people who take out their eyes ... this had such an impact on me! Later I went to film school at Temple University in Philadelphia. And in New York I went from film-making to reportage photography first, before I started working as a designer. Sometimes I think it's ironic that I'm mostly perceived as a writer today, because I see myself much more as an image-driven person.

Still, before you started your film festival, you launched your own blog, A Shaded View on Fashion. In 2005, you were among the very first generation of fashion bloggers.

Yes, for my blog I give a personal take on what I find interesting, not only in fashion, but without any limitations. It is my own shaded view that I share with my viewers. For a while I was also contributing to the websites of magazines like *Elle* or *Vogue*, but I noticed that there is a limit to how much you can speak about emerging talents and lesser-known labels there. And you have to make sure to always cover the advertisers. I didn't find that very appealing after a while …

In February 2013 Suzy Menkes published a controversial article in the New York Times entitled 'The Circus of Fashion'. In it, she claimed that many bloggers simply want to receive free trophy gifts. Shortly thereafter, you published a text via the blog Byronesque, which read like a reply to Menkes – and a defense of bloggers …

Well, I wrote my essay *Who Watches the Watchmen?* as a short history of fashion criticism, it wasn't meant as a reply to Suzy Menkes. In fact I wrote the text already in 2012, but then it took a while until it was published online. I always like reading Suzy Menkes, I respect her criticism a lot, and of course she's addressing an important issue here. She herself, as an editor of the *New York Times*, isn't allowed to accept any gifts, because that's the policy of the paper. And I think that's good. But the way I see it is that bloggers who write their content based on whoever is giving them presents or money are not better, or worse, than fashion magazines that only report on brands that buy their ad space. I think it's a double standard. You know, Chinese *Vogue* is turning down ads, their issues are heavy as phonebooks, 600 pages or more. And in *Vogue* there is an unspoken policy: if you place a one-page ad, you'll get a one-page editorial. That's why they have to refuse new ads! Things like this are rarely discussed – but bloggers get criticized all the time for being 'too uncritical', and they're asked to justify themselves for the fact that they, too, have to find ways of making money.

Diane Pernet in Paris, 2010

Your blog called a Fendi show 'boring', a Dolce & Gabbana show 'derivative' and a Gucci show 'soulless'. Aren't you afraid of being banned from the shows?

I'm sure that the labels are not very happy about the honesty, and it's true, if you don't give a good review you may not receive an invitation next time. But frankly, I'm not going crazy over it. As long as Rick Owens, Gareth Pugh and Dries Van Noten invite me to their shows, I'm fine. For my blog I work with a great photographer, Sonny Vandevelde, who takes beautiful backstage pictures at most fashion shows, so my viewers can have an impression of the shows I haven't seen myself.

Have you been banned by any label?

Well, here's an example: a couple of years ago I wrote a one-page feature on the Givenchy designer Riccardo Tisci and on Antony Hegarty, the singer of Antony and the Johnsons, for the Dutch fashion magazine *Zoo*. Shortly after its publication I came home and found a bouquet of flowers on my doorstep with a lovely note congratulating me on my film festival. That Christmas I received a beautiful black handbag from Givenchy and the following Christmas a beautiful jacket. I didn't know what I had done to deserve it. I hadn't asked for it! And then the next season I was given a front-row seat at the Givenchy show. So it went on for a few seasons. But then, suddenly, they gave me a last-row seat.

Probably you hadn't praised Givenchy enough on your blog?

I guess that was the problem. Kind of like: what have you done for us lately? So I sent an email to the Givenchy press office and said: 'If you're going to give me another crap seat at the next show you can just save your ticket. Keep the seat.' So they did. They didn't send me another invite.

Besides the internet and blogging: what would you say has changed most in the fashion business during the last 30 years?

One obvious difference is that in the past 15 years businessmen have become the most important figures in the fashion industry, and we have not been focusing on creative talent but creative business marketing instead. It's not easy for even a trained eye to tell the difference between many of the major brands' collections. They all look pretty much the same, and I find that is very sad.

Are there certain collections that you will never forget?

I'll always remember a Lanvin couture show that I attended right after I moved to Paris. Claude Montana was the designer at the time, and it was the most beautiful collection that I'd ever seen. Pure and sculptural. It made the hair stand up on my arms. It's a shame Montana isn't revered more today. A whole generation doesn't have a clue who he is – but he's a genius! Also, the first show that I saw of Walter Van Beirendonck literally blew me away. It was at the Lido, with masked models. That was in the 90s when Walter was sponsored by the German jeans brand Mustang and had the budget to truly express himself.

Could you see yourself working as a designer again at some point in the future?

By now I've seen too many collections in my life to be as pure and innocent as I think one needs to be as a designer. But who knows, maybe one day I'll bring out my own sunglasses collection? Actually I have been working on three scents recently: the owner of Intertrade Europe, a niche, luxury perfumes distributor from Italy, has offered to create scents with me. I want the first one to smell kind of serene and sort of green – not floral at all, but more like a walk through a forest.

... during which, I guess, you wouldn't take off your shades?

Probably not.

Charlie LE MINDU

HAIRSTYLIST
London

Once the wunderkind of the national hairstylists' academy in his native France, Charlie Le Mindu moved, after graduating, to Berlin, where he could be found cutting hair in clubs at night instead of at daytime salons. In 2009, Le Mindu moved on to London, where he makes gigantic handcrafted wig sculptures that take up to 500 hours to complete. These much-admired creations are jubilantly celebrated at Paris and London shows that are hardly distinguishable from parties. Born in Bergerac in the Dordogne in 1987, the inventive hair specialist has revived the art of 'haute coiffure' practically on his own, and does work for advertising productions, magazines, Lady Gaga, Grace Jones, Florence Welch and The B-52s. According to Le Mindu, hair is the new fur.

Monsieur Le Mindu, as an expert on hair, do you think that Anna Wintour, the editor of American Vogue, *wears a wig?*

No, she doesn't wear a wig, for sure. I guess people find it hard to believe that a woman of her age should have a bob that's naturally as voluminous as hers – she's over 60! But that doesn't mean it can't all be natural. I guess Anna Wintour's natural hair has always been very nice and thick, and she must take good care of it. Enough sleep, the right nutrition, excellent care products: all that works wonders for your hair.

What is poison for hair?

Drugs, of course. If you're high on speed all the time, well, that might be funny, but it has disastrous effects. Your hair is high on speed as well. Amphetamines make your hair grow much faster – and also your fingernails and toenails.

That's great for hairdressers!

Not at all. What's good about rapid growth when your hair has a really bad structure? I've seen it myself. Speed makes hair all dull and brittle. Hands off speed!

When did you start becoming interested in hair?

The first time I cut hair was when I was six: I was shaving my Barbie dolls bald. Then at 13, I really started to think about going into the world of coiffure and I trained on my family and friends. I gave all of them new haircuts. And then I did a five-year apprenticeship in Bordeaux. I have lots of diplomas from that time. But I guess you could say that my career really only took off in 2005 when I moved to Berlin …

… where you became known for your mobile salon, which opened in clubs at night.

Right. I never wanted to work in a standard salon because, you know, working in a daytime salon is really boring. In Bordeaux I used to work in a nice punk salon where we even did hair for dogs! But even the dogs got boring after a while. And even in the punk salon I got average customers who wanted their old-fashioned haircuts – and I had to listen to all their problems!

You don't enjoy moonlighting as a shrink?

I find it annoying. I mean, I understand why people tell their hairdresser their whole life story – it's quite an intimate situation having your hair and face touched all the time, which I guess loosens the tongue. But I'm a hairdresser because I like hair as material and I like to play around with its texture and volume – I didn't become a hairdresser to hear about other people's troubles. So it was fantastic when my friend Peaches suggested I open my mobile salon in her boyfriend's club, Rio, in Berlin. The music was very loud there, so you couldn't chat too much, and I got exactly the kind of client I wanted.

You mean drunks who took a spontaneous decision to have a party haircut and who basically agreed to everything you did to them?

No. I always tried to make sure that I only accepted people who weren't too drunk or

Models at Charlie Le Mindu's spring/summer 2010 show in London, September 2009

drugged out. They just had to be open-minded. I never had any problem – except for this one time: a girl who had really long, beautiful hair asked me to shave one side of her head. I did it, without realizing that she was off her face. She came back later and screamed: 'Why did you do it? Why did you do it!' Well, at least she was still laughing.

<u>Today, you live in London and cause quite a stir there with your so-called 'haute coiffure' and your collections of surreal wig sculptures.</u>

Well, I guess you could say that I'm not content with what I can do with my clients' hair. Not all of my clients let me go crazy. So when I do my wig sculptures, there are no restraints at all. I let my fantasy run riot. And there's another positive aspect: a wig sculpture won't just stay for one night, it stays there forever.

<u>Your sculptures remind me of everything from over-sized motorcycle helmets, to lips, to UFOs. How do you come up with these absurd shapes?</u>

I find inspiration in everything, really: by looking at animals, new technologies, things like aliens, or films by Tim Burton and David Lynch. The only thing I'm definitely not going to look at for inspiration are fashion magazines, never ever.

<u>Why not?</u>

Because I'm really scared to be unconsciously inspired by something that I may have seen in a fashion magazine. I do know how these magazines work – I've done hair for fashion shoots in *Dazed & Confused* or *i-D*, for example. These are great magazines, but they never feature anything that's really radical or future-oriented; everything still has to be market-compliant in some way. So if I were to draw my inspiration from fashion magazines, the result would turn out boring, I'm sure. I don't want that. That's why for one of my collections I decided to look into the architecture of towers – I let myself be inspired by the Eiffel Tower and by Lord Foster's so-called Gherkin in London. The Gherkin is quite nicely shaped, it's aerodynamic and it stands out so tall from the city. It's very sexual.

So you just put a giant dildo on the heads of your models?

Why not? Of course I'm not stupid: nobody's going to buy such a wig – or a toned down version of it – to wear out on the street. That's why my wigs are unique pieces; people can order them custom-made from me. And some of the pieces from my fashion shows I'll give to museums, like the Palais de Tokyo in Paris or the Boijmans Van Beuningen Museum in Rotterdam. The *Red Wall* from my first collection was part of the exhibition *The Art of Fashion* in Rotterdam, together with designs by Viktor & Rolf, Hussein Chalayan and Gareth Pugh.

If you don't sell many wig sculptures, how do you keep your business afloat?

I make money as a hairstylist for big advertisements and for television, and I work for music videos. I've done hair for The B-52s, Florence and the Machine, Lady Gaga and Grace Jones, or I've created wigs for them. And I have two sponsors – a brand that sells hair products, and an extension company – and they give me as much natural hair as I need for my sculptures.

So your sculptures aren't made from artificial hair?

Of course not! I don't like artificial hair. I only work with real human hair.

Where do these vast amounts of hair come from?

Looks from Charlie Le Mindu's spring/summer 2013 collection

From India and Eastern Europe. It's not unusual for women there to shave their heads and sell their hair. It might sound macabre, but for them it's a way to make a little extra money.

<u>There have been reports that, in the case of Indian temple hair, the profits don't go to the female pilgrims who donate their hair in Hindu temples, but that it's the middlemen in the temple organizations who make all the money.</u>

I'm quite sure that my sponsors don't use hair like that. But even if they do, I think it's still better to wear human hair than to wear fur and kill poor animals for it. I always say that hair is the new fur anyway.

<u>That's an impression one got from looking at runways in recent years: in their spring/summer 2009 show, Maison Martin Margiela presented a blonde hair coat, and Givenchy had skirts made of hair in one of their autumn/winter collections.</u>

Yes, and Sonia Rykiel used crimped red hair for coats, and in one collection by Jean-Charles de Castelbajac there was hair, too. Like I said: hair is the new fur. Obviously, Martin Margiela was the first to do it; he had been using hair for clothes for ages. Way before me! But to be honest, I never really looked at Margiela; I mean, I knew he was doing hair, but I wouldn't say that I was inspired by that or copied it. And I don't think that other designers used hair only because of Margiela. I think it's just a good time for a revival of hair in fashion. Even haute coiffure is coming back!

<u>What exactly is haute coiffure?</u>

I didn't invent that term. In the 1990s, when houses like Dior or Gaultier presented their haute couture collections, they made sure to not only show dresses, but matching hair-styles as well. It just went without saying that there would be crazy hair on the runway. But the designers stopped pushing it after a while. Maybe it was too expensive? Maybe they thought it was out of date? For a while, all you saw was short hair or slick, greasy hair. Everything was supposed to look as simple and 'natural' as possible. The grunge look. Then the Helmut Lang look. Basically, nobody wanted to look as if they had put a lot of effort into their hair. But these days are over, thank God!

<u>Hair also seemed to be in demand recently as an accessory: when Lady Gaga started her career, she wore a surrealistic 'hair bow' – a blonde bow-tie on her head, made from extentions.</u>

Well, I did like that, but Lady Gaga didn't come up with it herself. She copied it from people in London, or, to be precise, her stylist Nicola Formichetti copied it. A few years ago, he was hanging out at this club Boombox a lot, on Sundays in Shoreditch. All the fashion freaks went there. Boombox was all about dark wave music and haute couture. Everyone was wearing hair bows at Boombox. That's where Formichetti got the idea from. But I'm not disrespecting Lady Gaga – I often give my wigs to her. In her *Bad Romance* video, for example, she was wearing one of my blonde lip wigs, with an out-fit by Alexander McQueen. She put on the wig the wrong way around though, so you couldn't really see that it actually had the shape of huge lips.

<u>Do you still find the time to cut hair like a regular hairdresser, or are you much too busy creating your sculptures?</u>

Oh no, I still have people coming to my studio in Shoreditch, you know, friends and select customers. I have some lovely elderly ladies for example, from posh neighbour-

'I think it's just a good time for a revival of hair in fashion. Even haute coiffure is coming back!'

Blonde lip wig from the spring/summer 2010 collection.
Lady Gaga wore it back to front in her *Bad Romance* video in 2009.

hoods like Knightsbridge. Their chauffeurs drive them up to my studio – and off we go!

Could you explain why women always have to pay more for a haircut than men do?
Well, the traditional reasoning is of course that men's haircuts are less difficult, because men wear short hair.

But not every woman wears her hair long, and some men like to grow theirs.
I know. That's why when I had my mobile salon in Berlin, I had unisex prices: one cheaper rate for shorter hair, one more expensive rate for long hair – no matter whether boy or girl. But then I realized that there is a big difference, after all: boys know what they want, they'll tell me right away, 'I don't want a fringe', without hesitation. Girls are much more complicated. They want you to give them advice, they want to be persuaded. That's great on the one hand, because in the end girls are much more likely to experiment, but on the other hand it can take up to half an hour until they finally decide what kind of cut they want. And you know, waiting is a real pain in the ass. So the girls have to pay for that.

ZALDY

COSTUME DESIGNER
New York & Las Vegas

Without Zaldy Goco, many pop stars would look only half as brilliant or magical when they're on stage. Zaldy is counted among the top designers of glamorous, glittery – sometimes even electrically flickering – show outfits. From Lady Gaga and Britney Spears to Beyoncé and the Cirque du Soleil in Las Vegas, the Philippine-American has tailored costumes for seemingly everyone. The ones Zaldy designed for Michael Jackson's unrealized *This Is It* show are now on exhibition at museums. Before his career as a tailor for the stars took off, Zaldy enjoyed considerable success as an androgynous model. He then became the designer of his own prêt-à-porter line, which he presented for eight seasons in New York. He also served as chief designer for Gwen Stefani's L. A. M. B. label from 2004 to 2007.

Zaldy, what is the biggest challenge you face when designing stage costumes for pop stars?

Stage costumes need to read up close as well as from great distances, so they must be larger than life. They have to be more outrageous and exaggerated but also have to be quite detailed and intricate for when they are projected onto the screens. Striking a balance between the two extremes and ending up with something that looks stylish and not too costumey is always the challenge.

The costumes probably also have to be very comfortable?

Absolutely. Pop stars like Michael Jackson or Lady Gaga have to move, they are dancers and active performers. Their outfits need to be flexible like sportswear, even if sometimes they look quite sleek. Michael Jackson used to say: 'Everybody's got to learn their choreography, even the clothes have got to learn their choreography.' I always have to consider how an outfit is going to perform on stage. It's even more difficult if I have to incorporate harnesses and safety wires for acrobatics like in a Cirque du Soleil show, which is a whole other territory because, you know, these things are not small, they are quite bulky. So I try to figure out ways to work around practical challenges like these and still make an outfit aesthetically pleasing.

You made costumes for Michael Jackson's This Is It show in 2009 that ended up never being worn on stage because he passed away shortly before the premiere.

We did our last fitting with the costumes right before we were meant to leave for London. The costumes are part of the *This Is It* documentary. There is a special half-hour segment in the bonus material on the DVD where I show all the clothes and explain them. I haven't seen the segment myself – I don't like to watch myself! One day, maybe ten years from now, it will be fun to look at.

What happened to these costumes? Do you keep them in your archive?

No, I don't own them, they are owned by Michael Jackson's estate. They were paid for, you know. They have been travelling. They immediately went on tour as part of a Michael Jackson exhibition, to London, Tokyo and the Grammy Museum in Los Angeles. When I happened to be working in Japan in the summer of 2010, they were shown in Tokyo. Me and my whole team, we went and visited the clothes. We hadn't seen them since we put them on Michael for our last fitting. When we saw them on display, we were all in tears!

Did you talk to Michael Jackson about the stories behind some of his iconic looks during the run-up to the This Is It show – for example his white glove or the red Thriller leather jacket?

No, we never talked about that. The only thing I ever asked him was on the first day I met him. I looked down at his shoes and, you know, he wore the same type of black penny loafers that he always wore, so I said: 'Michael, hasn't anyone ever made you custom shoes?' He said 'No, not really' and that he wore them for practical reasons: they were the only shoes that allowed him to move the way he moved. And then he did a

Costumes and shoes by Zaldy
for Michael Jackson's
This Is It show, 2009

*'When Michael put
the pants on and the lights
switched on, he was speechless,
stunned. Finally he said:
"It's everything I've
always wanted!"'*

little moonwalk across the floor for me. I appeared very composed but I was freaking out on the inside!

<u>On the *This Is It* DVD you say you sent a pair of these penny loafers to Italy to have them reproduced by an Italian shoe manufacturer.</u>

Yes, I wanted someone to make shoes for Michael that looked different from the outside, but it was very important to make him feel on the inside that these were the exact same shoes he always wore. The people at the Italian factory had to cut open the left shoe to analyse them. They were terrified: 'These are Michael Jackson's shoes, we cannot destroy them!' But there was no way around it. We made him about ten styles with duplicates, which he loved!

<u>According to the DVD, the highlight of the *This Is It* show was to be a light-up *Billie Jean* suit. You made it using a new, illuminated, high-tech fabric called Lumalive.</u>

Yes, blinking socks, blinking legs, a blinking jacket and a blinking glove! Lumalive is a very advanced LED light made for performance by Philips Technology. It wasn't supposed to be ready for the market for a while, but as soon as we approached Philips they really pushed it and developed it just for Michael. You could run light effects on the outfit by remote control, almost like somebody playing a video game. I wish we had filmed the first fitting. When Michael put the pants on and the lights switched on, he was speechless, stunned. He didn't even say anything for like a minute, and finally he said: 'It's everything I've always wanted … It's everything I've always wanted!'

<u>So the suit had a power hook-up?</u>

No, it runs on pretty small batteries that are easy to hide in the outfit. Each element of the outfit had to have its own power source, you know, the glove had to be independent from the pants. It would arrive on stage in a suitcase, and then Michael would open up the suitcase and put on the glove and it was going to light up instantly.

<u>What did the insurance company say about the batteries?</u>

There really was no danger of electrocution. These batteries are harmless. I mean aside from exploding and leaking, but that's very unlikely.

<u>After the *This Is It* project you also made costumes for Lady Gaga's *Monster Ball* tour. Did she contact you in June 2009 right after Michael Jackson's death?</u>

No, I got the call a few weeks later. Originally it was going to be Gaga and Kanye West on tour together. I met them both in L.A. But then in September 2009 Kanye burst up on stage at the MTV Video Music Awards and cut into Taylor Swift's acceptance speech. It became a huge scandal and then within one week I got word that the tour was cancelled and that Lady Gaga would push forward doing just a Gaga tour. Everything had to happen in practically no time – you know, in 2009 she became more and more iconic by the day; she rose faster than anybody you have ever seen become famous! I never did costumes faster than for the *Monster Ball*. My favourite one was a gold-studded Egyptian outfit that we did. It looked like metal, but it was custom-made leather that I got from this incredible company in Spain. All of the studs were gold-plated and we studded the entire outfit.

<u>Did you always know that you wanted to work with clothes?</u>

I think so, yes. As far as I can remember I was allowed to choose my own clothes to buy. Later on I became the unofficial stylist of the family. Everyone always asked my opin-

Zaldy in his New York studio, 2011

ion, if they should buy this or what they should wear. I was meant to be a doctor, like everyone else in the family, but I insisted I had to go to art school. Finally they gave in and I went to both Parsons and F.I.T. in New York. Years later I would go on to do eight seasons of my own line and at the same time design seven seasons of L.A.M.B. with Gwen Stefani. But, before all that the runway called and somehow I became a model! Really, I don't know how I did any of it; I don't really like being the center of attention.

<u>Well, how did you become a model?</u>

It all happened by fate. After I graduated I met Thierry Mugler and I wanted to work with him in Paris. I went to interview with him and a few other designers, but people said: 'Why do you want to be a designer? You should be a model!'

<u>Were you insulted?</u>

A bit, as I was very serious about becoming a designer. But it was also sort of flattering and I just went with the flow. I modelled as both a boy and as a girl. I did runway for Jean Paul Gaultier, Vivienne Westwood, Thierry Mugler and more. My first photo shoot was with Steven Meisel and then Steven Klein and Karl Lagerfeld, Ellen von Unwerth, Glen Luchford and so many amazing photographers ... In 1995 I even did this Levi's commercial that was sort of infamous at the time: I sit in the back of a taxi cab, dressed as a sexy woman, and then I get a razor from my bag and start shaving my chin – the driver, eyeing me in the rear-view mirror, almost has a heart attack! It was quite a scandal at the time. It was banned in France until after 9 pm!

<u>You mean today there wouldn't be a scandal anymore?</u>

Well, I think gender and sex are becoming more demystified today, not only in fashion. It's not about secrets anymore. Now there's Lea T. in Givenchy campaigns, you know, an intersex model who's amazingly feminine, and there's Andrej Pejic, an Eastern

European boy who looks just like a beautiful blonde woman. He does Marc Jacobs ads. I don't know, maybe the designers are still trying to push these things as a sensation, but they aren't so sensational anymore – they've become very public. Cathy Horyn wrote an amazing story about this in the *New York Times*, its title was 'Pushing Boundaries That No Longer Exist'. Anyway, for me, being a special model in the 90s and getting to see this side of the industry was an interesting experience – participating in how garments are sold down the runway and understanding what it means to make a lasting image. It helped me a lot professionally.

Is it true that you designed your very first stage costume for Lady Miss Kier, the singer of Deee-Lite?

Yes, that was when I was still a student in New York. I was going to parties quite a lot at the time and I always wore new, crazy outfits I had made for myself. So Lady Miss Kier saw me out in the club and I guess she liked the way I looked. She came up to me and asked me if I could make her a version of the mirrored outfit that I had designed for myself. It was studded all over with small pieces of mirror I had cut from a plastic mirror; it was kind of a futuristic catsuit. Even the shoes were built in. I loved Deee-Lite, so how could I say no? She even wanted me to be her synchronized dance partner, which I did for a second but, as you know, I like to be behind the scene!

Lady Miss Kier seems to have kicked off quite a few fashion careers: Jeremy Scott says he only got the idea to become a designer after he participated in a competition to design new platform shoes for Lady Miss Kier. He didn't win the competition, but he won the confidence that he could be a designer ...

Really? I love that!

Zaldy at work in his studio, 2011

Willi NINJA

RUNWAY COACH
New York

No other personality moved more graciously between the fashionable mainstream and gay subculture than Willi Ninja. Born William Leake in New York in 1961, Ninja is regarded as the most legendary of voguers. In this dance style, which emerged from the queer Afro-American and Latin American ball tradition in Harlem, fashion poses from *Vogue* are presented in acrobatic choreographies. Ninja toured the world with Malcom McLaren and his own vogueing show even before Madonna popularized the style with her hit song 'Vogue' (1990). During the same period, Ninja worked as a model (for Thierry Mugler, among others) and as a runway coach. Naomi Campbell, Paris Hilton and many others copped their glamorous hip swings from him. This interview with the underground icon was conducted in New York in late 2005. Ninja died in September 2006.

Mr. Ninja, when did you start vogueing?

Oh, that must have been in the late 70s when I used to go to clubs a lot, the black gay clubs in the Village like Peter Rabbit's and The Cockring, and dance my ass off. One night I saw two people vogueing, but it was bad, so I paid them no mind. Then somebody came after me and said: 'Don't you realize this guy is challenging you?' I said: 'What? How do you know?' And he said: 'Because he's vogueing and he's looking directly at you!' And I said: 'Vogue?' So I kept on doing my regular dancing, just like I danced at the time, and blew him o–u–t!

So that was your first vogueing battle, without even knowing it …

Exactly. And then I heard about Hector Xtravaganza, the creator of the House of Xtravaganza. Everybody was telling me 'You gotta see Hector! You gotta see Hector!' He had a sense of timing … it was unbelievable. Especially if he had a prop. It could be a cane or a scarf, a blanket or a hat, whatever. Oh, he knew how to work the hat! Plus he had a little ballet background, so he would incorporate that and do different things. Hector died in 85. I don't care what anybody says, to me he was the best ever. I haven't seen anybody vogue better since. Normally Hector wouldn't show anyone anything, but I said 'Pleeeeease, I've been hearing about you for so long!' And there was something he liked about me. So he worked with me for a bit. That was in 81. And I created my style with a little bit of his after that.

So you never had a professional dance education like ballet?

No. You know, I always wanted to take ballet classes, but not in my neighbourhood! I come from Flushing, Queens and let me tell you, you don't want to get caught or busted there. I was too scared. To grow up in the ghetto and not be masculine but very feminine, you gotta watch out, your ass is in trouble!

The first vogueing houses must have been founded already in the late 60s …

Yes, way before me! I think the House of Omni was the first house, Kevin Omni started it. House of Pendavis and House of LaBeija must have been there right from the start, too. I mean they were always having drag balls in Harlem, but then in the 60s it shifted a little, because, you know, not everybody likes to dress as a woman, not everybody does drag. So they added all sorts of different categories at the balls, for example for butch men, for school kids, for all sorts of crazy costumes.

Dressing up and fashion seem to have been very important not only when the first houses were formed, but also when vogueing was developed.

Definitely. In the beginning it was all about taking the models' moves and poses from fashion magazines and putting them to music, you know, dance them to the breaks of disco songs. So it was 'Vogue'. It just wouldn't have sounded right if we had said 'Let's do the *Bazaar*!' or 'Show me the *Esquire*.' So …

Many houses have fashion names, like House of St. Laurent, House of Miyake-Mugler, House of Vuitton. Didn't the fashion houses ever complain or sue?

Oh yes, Chanel once sued, so the House of Chanel had to change their name. They said they would change it to House of Chanel International, so they put an 'International' behind. And I think it was also – was it Givenchy? I can't remember exactly who else was suing, but the high fashion houses don't play! Which is silly, because the vogueing houses don't advertise or sell anything, you know. There are new houses now. There's the House of Latex, House of Allure … there are so many new ones I can't even keep track!

It seems that a lot of the people in the ball community, all they live for and all they spend their money on is balls and costumes …

Yes, they're expensive. I mean I myself wear skirts, little short skirts, kilts, or long dresses, but just the bottom part of the dress. The upper part is usually masculine. And if I have my goatee and my long hair, it's almost like … People don't get that I'm not in drag, I'm just me. But you're right, today in the ballroom scene it's a lot about real designer labels. Especially the shoes and eyewear. I don't know how these bitches do it – if they have bad credit cards or what. All I know is they walk in at the balls with Christian Dior, Chanel, Gucci, the real ones! We're talking the most expensive. No fakes! They even bring the receipts, just in case somebody doubts it.

In this respect ball culture seems to have parallels with hip-hop culture: it's about showing what you've got and what you've achieved …

Right, there are some parallels. But there's also a big difference: our culture never made it big – because it's a gay thing. There's never been a niche for us. So we have to push our way in somewhere. That's where our ambition comes from.

In 1989 you co-wrote lyrics for Malcolm McLaren's Waltz Darling album and you also starred prominently in his Deep in Vogue video, which was the first music video to present vogueing to a larger public. How did this collaboration come about?

That was because of Patricia Field.

The fashion designer from New York?

Yes, she's my gay mother. Pat believed in me and my talent for so long and she kept trying to get people to take me on, so in 1988 she threw the 'Field Ball'. I was supposed to open the vogue category, demonstrate it, and I was also judging. It was an all-celebrity panel and Pat sat me between Mary McFadden, who was one of New York's top designers at the time, and Malcolm McLaren. So Malcolm and I were talking, and when the ball started and it came to the vogue category, I demonstrated the dance. After that Malcolm came to me and said: 'I want to talk to you! Can you choreograph a video for me?' I said: 'Sure!' Then he called me later: 'Can you be in the video?' I said: 'Yeah!' A few days later he called me again: 'Er, can you also write the song?'

Wow, he really was after you!

I know!

'Chanel once sued, so the House of Chanel had to change their name. And I think it was also – was it Givenchy? I can't remember exactly who else was suing, but the high fashion houses don't play!'

Willi Ninja, shot by Mark Baker for the cover of Malcolm McLaren's single 'Deep in Vogue' (1989)

<u>And do you know how Madonna got involved with vogueing a little later?</u>
What happened was, Lauren Hutton – who was engaged to Malcolm McLaren at the time – and Madonna were very good friends. So Lauren brought Madonna to the editing of the 'Deep in Vogue' video when Malcolm and I were in the cutting room working on it. And then Madonna asked me and Adrian, the other dancer in the video, to perform with her at a benefit she was organizing. So we did that, and then she wanted me and Adrian on her *Blond Ambition* tour as dancers, because she loved that we were like Ying and Yang – he's light, I'm dark. But I had to say no.

Willi Ninja, shot by Christian Siekmeier (2006)

Why?

Because I was dancing for Malcolm already and he was giving me equal billing on his tour. Imagine if I had worked for Madonna! When you become one of her dancers, it's like you're not existing, you just backdrop! Plus I'm not technically trained as a dancer. I mean I do a fierce job, but I can't compete with professional jazz or ballet dancers, for example when it comes to certain spins. So I went the route that I knew and did the smaller thing. And Malcolm was so funny, that's why we clicked. You know, for example the press put in the paper that I was his new lover. The headline was 'What happened to Lauren?' I asked him: 'Aren't you gonna do anything about this?' And he said: 'Eh, any publicity is good publicity!' And I said: 'Maybe that's okay for you, but not for me, you're not my taste!'

The years 1990 and 1991 must have been very exciting for you, with vogueing suddenly being the hottest thing around the world …

Yes, I mean vogueing was huge in Europe, and in the gay clubs in the US, too. I even met a guy from Wisconsin who told me: 'Oh, vogueing is huge there!' I was like: 'Wisconsin?!' And in Japan, I was such a huge star there, it was almost ridiculous. I didn't even have to release any new songs. I stayed on top for about five years there.

Did you spend time in Japan?

Oh yes, in Sendai, north of Tokyo. I lived there for four months and had a great time! I was running a club and doing vogueing shows, and I was teaching courses for Japanese women who wanted to learn how to behave when they travel, to build their confidence. I told them: 'You cannot go to a foreign country and have your head down all the time, because you look like a victim. Keep your head up, be proud! I'm not stopping you from your real culture. Your husband still may have to walk slightly in front of you, I know – but keep your head up!'

Teaching women how to walk, that's how you acquired the name 'Willi Ninja – the Walking Man'.

Right, that came from being a runway coach. Because besides J. Alexander I'm one of the best. I've worked with a loooot of models over the years, and I've been doing it for almost 30 years now. It's fun, especially if I'm working with the big girls, big names. But I also love my big girls, you know, plus-size models. They are so sweet and they try so hard! Not like the size zero girls who think they're fierce already and give me attitude!

Don't the models ever find it strange that they are taught by a man?

You know, I always have my pumps with me, so I can show them that I can do it in heels, too! Sometimes I even have to physically show them, like grab their feet, lead them and stop them. That's how I got two high heel scars on my hands …

How did you learn walking?

Oh, as a kid I loved watching classic films. I watched Audrey Hepburn, she was so amazing! I love all the old films when women were women. They were tough, you know, but they were also soft, watching their hand movements and the way they moved. And if they had little fashion shows in the movies, I studied the fashion shows, the different turns. Also I used to sit by the big Betamax screens at Bloomingdale's, watching the fashion shows, especially Iman, the first black top model. That's how I learned to walk. I teach the models everything. Whenever there's a new trend on the runway, they learn that from me, too. I keep up, because things change. You know, some years ago they used to like the girls to do the pony walk, when they lift their knees so high they're walking like a horse. I hated that walk, it's not ladylike! I've never met a woman in my life who walks like a trampling horse pulling a beer wagon. And then the attitude is important, of course … You know, when I think of sensuality if I want to walk as a female, I think of 'Lola', the Sarah Vaughan song: 'Whatever Lola wants, Lola gets!'

Is it true that you also taught Naomi Campbell?

Yes, I worked with the cow. I mean, she and I were good friends, and she already knew how to walk. People think I taught her how to walk, but no, I taught her how to juice it up! If you saw her on the runway in 1989, she had a great walk already, but it was kind of normal. Then all of a sudden in 1990, the 'Super Strut'!

The 'Super Strut'?

Yes, that became her signature walk for a while. She learned that from me, Adrian Xtravaganza and Connie Girl, a drag queen who used to battle and whom we used to show Naomi.

Naomi Campbell copied her strut from a drag queen?

Yes, there's a funny story: when Thierry Mugler was directing George Michael's 'Too Funky' video in 92, with Tyra Banks, Linda Evangelista and all those super models, he also put Connie Girl in the video. Everybody thought it was Naomi. You see a black cowgirl walking on the runway, you see her back. Cowboy hat, little tight bikini top and cut-off jeans shorts with fringes hanging off. Same hair colour as Naomi, same body shape, same strut. But it's not Naomi, it's a boy – you just never see his face! I thought it was hysterical. Connie Girl could walk her ass off, she could literally walk rings around Naomi.

Do you coach men as well?

I do, but that's easy. You might look at me and say 'How can you?', but trust me, I can change! Guys have only two different walks: normal, casual, that fits for suits and regular gear; and you have the urban hip-hop walk for the street wear – but you don't want to do it too hard! When I teach guys, I say: 'You need to feel what the clothes give you. If it's masculine clothes, you can be very masculine; if it's sexy clothes, you need to be sensual when you walk. But it's not only the walk, it's also how you look. Don't do stupid things with your mouth! Close your lips and then let them slowly part, to give the women that sexy look.' Minor things, really simple things!

One might wonder why you – even though you're not doing drag – call yourself 'Mother' of your House of Ninja, instead of 'Father' …

That's because fathers often just run away from life. Mothers are much stronger. Not only do mothers take care of the family, they also work, they do the double job. A male figure is only going to work, he's not going to do the duties at home. And women take pain better. My mom was my inspiration. She's in a wheelchair but she always took good care of me and my two sisters – they're my first cousins actually, but she took them in after their mother died of cancer. My mother raised the three of us almost on no money, making sure that we could go to the movies and museums, were well dressed and well fed, and she educated us. My mother is a very strong woman.

Willi Ninja, shot by Christian Siekmeier (2006)

Yes, there are twelve Houses of Ninja altogether. I've got chapters in Miami, Washington, Chicago, Baltimore, Atlanta and so on. I think altogether we've got about 200 members. It varies. So far we've done pretty good. I only had to shut down Washington once. The Father of the house told all those kids to come to the 'Balenciaga Ball', and some of them had to dish out money to get in the ball, but basically he had nowhere for them to stay. So I said: 'No such thing!' And I had to close down Virginia once for a scandal. The young man who was running the house wasn't going to school, and then I saw him on something like an escort service website. I didn't want that!

No, you don't have to dance, you can pick any ball category you want. Or, if we like you enough, you can just be an honorary member, just carry the name without taking part in the balls. You don't even have do be gay. The Father of my house in New York is straight. He's a 6-foot-4 Jamaican, ripped, his name is Archie. I taught him how to do runway, male and female, and I also taught him how to vogue. He's a bodybuilder type, but he can also cut it up the other side. He's very secure about himself, he doesn't give a fuck what anybody says, he says: 'Vogueing is an artform, I love to dance.' Which he really does. Don't go to a club with Archie, you can't hang, he'll be on the dance floor from the time he gets there until the place closes! Just like I used to in the late 70s. Back then I would go to the clubs to dance, dance, dance and do whatever the latest thing was, find out everything. If you ask me, those kids are usually the best dancers – who learn everything in the clubs, who watch the other kids like a hawk and then go home and practise. You can take ballet classes later, if you want ...

Pierre *CARDIN*

FASHION DESIGNER
Paris

Known as the 'king of licensing' and the 'pioneer of prêt-à-porter', Pierre Cardin was born Pietro Cardin in San Biagio di Callalta, Italy, in 1922. Cardin started out working for the haute couture houses Paquin, Dior and Schiaparelli, before opening his own house in 1950. When nine years later he began selling prêt-à-porter, the Paris Chambre Syndicale was so insulted that they threw him out (only to reinstate him later). In the 1960s, Cardin's futuristic geometric line defined the characteristic Space Age look, while his global licensing deals soon brought to the market items like furniture, frying pans and record players – all with the same Space Age style. This interview took place at Cardin's headquarters in the Rue du Faubourg Saint-Honoré, where the sprightly senior still runs the show.

Monsieur Cardin, it's said that you plan to sell your company for a total of one bil-lion euros.

That's correct. I'd like to pass my company on to somebody. I'm now well over 80 years old. A man at my age must think of the future! Who knows how long I'll be able to carry on like this? If I were only 50 or 60 I'd certainly not want to sell. Business is boom-ing – as you know.

Are there any potential purchasers?

Nothing is definite yet. A billion euros for the name Pierre Cardin is a lot of money, of course. But we're talking about the rights to my brand throughout the whole world. Who knows, perhaps I should be asking for more. If you can charge a lot for some-thing – it's a good thing.

Why is your brand worth a billion euros?

Because I've been in the business for so long; that's the main reason. I haven't just been around for 20 years like many of the others. I started as a very young man – I was 20 when I entered the fashion business. That's almost 70 years ago, can you imagine! Nobody's been at it longer than I have. And, more importantly, I'm a professional. As well as designing clothes, I'm also a businessman. I always was. That's because I worked for the Red Cross for three years in Paris during the Second World War. Part of my job was to deal with money, and that's where I learned how important it is to spend only your own money. In my entire life I've never run up any debts, nor have I ever sold any shares in my company. That means that today I'm lucky enough not to belong to Monsieur Pinault and his huge company.

You mean PPR?

Precisely. Nor is my firm part of Bernard Arnault's LVMH Group. I have no partners; my company isn't listed; here, everything belongs to me. One hundred percent. My money, my house, my name, my talent.

Not forgetting your prêt-à-porter fashion.

That, of course, is the most important reason why my company is worth so much money. I was the first couturier to have the idea of selling prêt-à-porter fashion. When

'If everybody keeps saying that Pierre Cardin produces the most visionary designs, you will want to own at least a pair of socks by him. Communication is everything.'

Pierre Cardin coat, 1959

I started doing it in 1959 and my designs were hanging on sales racks in department stores all over the world, from Printemps to Takashimaya and Harrods, people said: 'Pierre Cardin has lost his mind; in three years he'll be finished'. In fact, what I did was really rather vulgar for the times. But I asked myself: Why should I only dress wealthy, middle-class women when I could actually dress all women? I was already successful with my haute couture beforehand, but it was through prêt-à-porter that I made my fortune – and with the licences of course.

They call you the 'king of licences'. In your own words, what exactly is a licence?
A licence is a means to sell my name. Like Coca-Cola, all over the world. I permit some-one to use my name and logo, and he pays me to do so. But that doesn't mean I just grab the money – I work for it as well. I still draw my licensed collections myself. I send all my licensees drawings I make, 50 of them, twice a year – that's one hundred Pierre Cardin drawings per year! Shirts, coats, shoes, bags, and so on. I have licensees in 140 countries throughout the world, and I have visited every single country. Alaska, New Zealand, Argentina, China, I was everywhere. Ireland, Stockholm, Germany, Spain. Japan is the country I've visited most frequently; I've been there 102 times altogether. I've shown my collections in the Senso-ji Temple in Tokyo, by the Pyramids of Giza, and on Red Square in Moscow.

You say that by introducing prêt-à-porter you democratized fashion. When you think about how expensive haute couture is, that seems plausible. But isn't demo-cratic fashion – created by a fashion designer whose role seen in a historical perspective could certainly be compared with that of an absolute ruler – a contradiction?

Of course not! It's a question of being creative. If I lacked the talent to design fashion, there wouldn't be anything to democratize, my company would have closed down long ago. But Pierre Cardin has survived to the present day because my collections stand out and because they're interesting from a cultural point of view. The power of the creator is what counts. Of course this power cannot be democratized. Fashion, on the other hand, can – if everyone can afford it.

Items sold under your name have included perfumes, frying pans, aircrafts, houses, fabrics ...

... and cars, Champagne and even chocolate! 45 years ago I designed a package for chocolate. It was round and silver and looked highly futuristic, like a Sputnik. The French chocolatiers found the packaging ludicrous, but I won a design prize for it nonetheless.

Is there anything you can't design?

Hmm ...

You once said you could even imagine designing Pierre Cardin toilet paper.

I said that to the magazine *Harper's Bazaar*, a very long time ago. I had designed some pink hygienic tissue paper. Carmel Snow, the elitist editor-in-chief of *Harper's*, said to me that she couldn't understand how I could do anything as vulgar as that. I didn't know what she meant. Everyone needs paper tissues. Every day we're pleased that paper tissues exist. Of course, if you use designer tissues it's rather sad to throw them away afterwards. But what's vulgar about that? How is perfume any different? Perfume is also used for grooming; it's a prestigious product, people spend a lot of money on it, and if possible it should be from a famous designer. So why shouldn't there be designer tissue paper – or indeed designer toilet paper?

One of your most successful licensed products is socks. If you put yourself in the place of a purchaser, why should someone choose to wear a pair of socks by Pierre Cardin rather than by some other brand, say Bonprix?

Because I'm Pierre Cardin and people know me. During the 60 years of my career there have been many covers and interviews and photo shoots with me. If you want to establish a

Water-repellent space-age look, 1990

name for yourself, you need to make sure you're talked about frequently; constant repetition and reminders are important. When you keep hearing that there's a great film playing in cinemas, you'll want to see that film yourself. That's how fashion functions, too: if everybody keeps saying that Pierre Cardin produces the most visionary designs, you'll want to own at least a pair of socks by him. Communication is everything. The only difference is that I have never paid for it.

You mean advertising?

No, editorial pages. All the really big design houses in Paris purchase reports in the fashion magazines. They pay for their publicity. I don't do that – I never have! I don't spend my money on publicity; I prefer to spend it on culture. For example, I have my own theatre in Paris, the Espace Pierre Cardin, and I stage musicals there. The press can write about them, and that's also publicity for me.

So you control your image. Can you also control the quality of your licensed products?

I try to. But you know, licences are like your own children. You have maybe ten of them and of course you would like to look after them all equally. But that's not always possible. Some of them may be different from the rest of the family, some of them may be crazy, some of them turn out wonderful and they even look good. I have, if you like, 400 children to take care of. It's inevitable that not all of them are top quality.

But if a licensed product turns out differently from the rest, is it still a true Cardin?

Of course!

In an interview with the fashion magazine *Fantastic Man,* you said on the subject of licences that the backlash was inevitable.

We were talking about the 1980s. At that time there really were problems with licensees, but I never reduced my licensing business for that reason. I just made sure that I found better licence partners and improved the quality that way.

So have you never made any mistakes in your life?

Of course I have! I could have collaborated on plastic watches with Swatch. Swatch wanted to negotiate a huge contract with me, but I wasn't interested. Or trainers: I had the chance to go into partnership with Nike. My staff advised me against it. They said: 'Trainers are vulgar, don't stoop to that sort of thing.' And the same thing with jeans. The fact that I didn't move into the jeans market at an early stage was perhaps the biggest mistake of my life. Today, everyone wears designer jeans. Unfortunately, my staff advised me against that, too. Since then, I've never listened to anybody, I make my own decisions. If I make a mistake today, it will be my own. I prefer my own mistakes to other people's, you know.

Let's talk about the image of women that you created in the late 1950s with your prêt-à-porter. It was revolutionary.

Yes, I designed fashion for the working woman from the very beginning. Don't forget that in those days haute couture was a much more bourgeois affair than it is today. Haute couture customers were women who didn't work. They had a chauffeur, a nanny and all sorts of things. But the emancipated working woman, who fought for her independence, interested me far more.

Leather man, 1995

How would you describe your designs for this new type of woman?

As simple and as flexible as possible. My outfits didn't include high heels, hats with huge brims or stiff, sweeping skirts. My fashion had nothing classically feminine about it; it was modern fashion, in which women could drive cars, go to the cinema or travel by air. My designs were elegant, but not complicated. Above all, they had no frills or anything like that. I wanted to reflect the new realities of life at that time.

Shortly afterwards you also became very influential in men's fashion.

Initially it was an insult that I even started designing fashion for men in 1960. There had never been anything like it – a couturier who dressed not only women, but men as well!

Were the men afraid that they might be made to look effeminate by a women's designer? Your men's fashion was tight-fitted and considered to be quite sexy.

That's possible. But if the image of women was undergoing change, then surely men's image needed to change as well. And apart from that, I had to compete. In those days it was mainly the classic Italian and English men's tailors who set the tone in men's fashion. So I had to come up with something new. I phoned all the universities in Paris and got them to send me 30 young students of mathematics, philosophy and medicine. I designed my fashion for these boys – they were all 18 or 19 years old – and then I had them present it at the Hôtel de Crillon on Place de la Concorde. It was revolutionary. *The New York Times* wrote about it on its front page: a triumph!

It's all the more surprising to see how innovative your approach was in those days when you consider that, in fact, you started out in the classic couture system: your career began in 1944 as a fashion draughtsman in the house of Jeanne Paquin.

Yes, Paquin was one of the best haute couture houses in Paris in the 1940s. At that time, the company had 1,200 employees for couture alone! It's impossible to imagine that these days: there was a salon, a *femme de chambre*, a salon de thé – the customers came, stayed for eight days and ordered maybe 50 to 60 items each season. Dressing gowns, evening gowns, cocktail dresses and so on. Everything was made to measure and the women had to come for several fittings. All this went down twice a year. What a fuss!

After Paquin you then worked for the legendary Elsa Schiaparelli.

I worked for her for only three months. At the time, Schiaparelli had just returned from New York, where she had lived in exile during the Second World War. I started at her house because she was known for this

Pointed pagoda shoulders for men, 1979

The new, provocatively slim men's line by Cardin, 1960

Surrealist shoe hat, which looked like a pump that had been put upside down on some-one's head. Salvador Dalí had designed it for her in 1937. Schiaparelli produced the most amusing fashion at the time. I was young and enjoyed the fun.

Before you finally opened your own house in 1950, you worked for Christian Dior for three years. He's regarded as having been your greatest patron. Why did you not become his successor, instead of Yves Saint Laurent, when Dior died unexpectedly in October 1957?

When Dior died I had already established my own house. Should I have closed it again? Of course not. But Dior did indeed support me strongly. In 1949, for example, he introduced me to Robert Piguet. Piguet was the son of a highly regarded Swiss banking family and ran a large couture house on the Champs Élysées, with 400 employees. Dior thought I could become his successor, since Piguet was unable to work at that stage because he had cancer. But I still preferred to open my own house. Piguet closed his in 1951, and two years later he died.

What are your memories of your time with Christian Dior?

Oh, he was a great gourmand. He sucked sweets all the time, almost poured them down his throat. Munch, munch, munch all day long. That's what killed him. My God, he really did eat too much! Apart from that, he was a very charming and cultivated man. Very discreet and warm-hearted. But nonetheless it was really the golden era of Cristóbal Balenciaga – in my opinion, at least. Balenciaga had even more personality than Dior.

Allegedly you would have liked to work for Balenciaga.

'Dior sucked sweets all the time. Munch, munch, all day long. That's what killed him. My God, he really did eat too much!'

Elegance à la Cardin, 1962

Yes, after my three months with Schiaparelli I really wanted to work for him. I had a very high opinion of Balenciaga at that time because of his costumes and coats, not so much for his evening gowns. But I was unlucky. His directress was very aggressive and arrogant, she wouldn't let anyone get near him. I went there three times to introduce myself, and three times she sent me away. Later, when I met Cristóbal Balenciaga personally, he said to me: 'Really? You wanted to work for me? I would have been delighted!' But after the third time I couldn't be bothered anymore. So I went to Dior. Voilà!

Uniforms for future female moonwalkers, 1968

You weren't accepted by Balenciaga then, but nonetheless you seem to have made your mark on the house. Suzy Menkes, the world's leading fashion journalist, detected a futuristic Cardin influence in Nicolas Ghesquière's collection for Balenciaga in the Paris fashion shows for the autumn/winter season 2010.

Really? Well, the things I designed 50 years ago are still ultramodern today.

Does that mean that the world today really does look as futuristic as you imagined it 50 years ago?

Absolutely. As a young man, I used to dream about how, in the future, man would land on the moon. I dreamed of computers and of how we would no longer walk along the sidewalk, but would roll on it. I formulated all these things using the resources of fashion. And all of them became reality.

But you also predicted on one occasion that in the future no one would wear ties anymore.

That was a misunderstanding. What I said was that in the future no one would wear ties anymore if the president carried on like that.

If the president carried on like what?

I was talking about that Socialist in the 1980s. What was his name again? Mitterrand. At the time, I had sold an incredible number of Pierre Cardin ties. If they had all been stitched together, the tie would have been long enough to go around the world twice. You can work out yourself how many ties that must have been. A tie is about one and a half metres long … so?

Hmm, that makes about 27 million ties?

Something like that. But then Mitterrand came along and said: 'With or without a tie – what difference does it make?' So after that, the sales of ties in France sank rapidly, the economy started to struggle and entire factories were closed. Thousands of workers were reduced to poverty. And all that simply because of the stupidity of that Socialist! I used to have three tie factories. Now I only have one.

Damir DOMA

FASHION DESIGNER
Paris

The swift rise of Damir Doma was – in the recent history of fashion – unprecedented. In just six years, Doma went from Paris Fashion Week debutant to the owner of his first flagship store in the Rue du Faubourg Saint-Honoré. The label's success is attributable not only to its smart, androgynous, purist, sensual aesthetic – an aesthetic beloved by Lenny Kravitz and Robert Pattinson, to name a few – but also to the fact that, in the background, everything works in concert. Born in Virovitica, Croatia, in 1981, and raised in Bavaria, Doma's own mother is a master seamstress and makes his patterns in her studio in Traunstein; business matters are attended to by his partners from the Paper Rain Group. Initially a menswear designer, Doma presented his first women's collection in 2010.

Damir Doma, how many collections do you design per year?

Two men's collections, two women's collections, two pre-collections and then again two men's and women's collections for my Silent line. That makes a total of ten collections per year.

That's crazy!

Yes, it's a lot of work. If I were sick for two or three weeks it would be virtually impossible to make up the lost time. The whole thing requires organization and a team of good people. Some people imagine that success just happens if you're talented. But above a certain level all fashion designers have talent, and then it's really a question of discipline and hard work.

Do you still know the names of all your employees?

There aren't that many of them; we're a team of about 20. But the company is growing relatively fast and so we have to expand our structure. That means I have to learn to delegate more. The problem is that fashion doesn't work in a democratic way. There has to be someone who says what's what. And then all the others have to toe the line. It's important that I set out clear guidelines, and then on the level below me it's all a matter of teamwork.

Do you have certain rituals for calming yourself down when things get stressful?

I like to go running. When I was young I did a lot of sport, but today it fulfils a different purpose. In those days it was a question of spending time with my friends. Nowadays I need sport in order to be able to switch off. Running is a sort of meditation. Or if I want to think about something else I take the afternoon off and go to see an exhibition at the Centre Pompidou.

Which is only five minutes' walk away from your studio ...

That's how I clear my head. I have certain rituals when I'm in my studio, too. For example, at the beginning of each new season I start a new mood book in which I collect everything that gives me inspiration – photos, drawings, pictures. Then I send the book to all the creative people who work with me. My assistants have a copy, and even the DJ who works on the music for the show gets one. The book links us all together. And it helps me to get through the season. Because a great deal happens in six months; I'm constantly exposed to new influences – it's all too easy to lose my way. The mood book is the framework that I set for myself.

What framework have you set for the Damir Doma aesthetic?

The main themes behind Damir Doma are purism and sensitivity.

One could get the impression that it's also about avoiding vulgarity.

Probably sensitivity and purism automatically exclude something like vulgarity? Indeed, if I have a feeling that something is vulgar I won't allow it. But it's very hard to pin down exactly when something is vulgar.

Vulgarity in the way Versace uses it, for example, doesn't exist in your work – garish colours, offensive sexuality …

That would be contradictory to my character. I find that sort of thing common. In my collections it's often a question of finding the balance between opposites. Especially in the men's collections. If I use softish influences there, for example in a jacket that's very flowing, I'll balance it out elsewhere – for example by combining the outfit with sturdy shoes.

It's often pointed out how your men's collections consist of flowing layers and how little use you make of the classic man's wardrobe: padded shoulders, jackets, stiff collars – you rarely work with such details.

Classic men's fashion comes from uniforms; it has its origins in the military. I find it very aggressive and static. The classic suit is very structured, especially at the front, where it almost looks like a suit of armour. I think this sort of clothing often looks more like a disguise. My approach is that the inside and outside should blend together to form a whole.

So if your menswear doesn't give the man poise through its cut and structure, then the man must provide the poise himself?

Of course it takes confidence to wear clothing like this. As much as it can require a rejection of the standard – a refusal to conform and to obey dictates. Clothing is always communication and an expression of personality. That, for me, is actually the most interesting aspect of fashion: that everyone can use it to express himself or herself. There are not many other ways of doing that. Not everyone can sing, and not everyone can paint or dance. But everyone dresses.

In fact, padded shoulders are used more frequently in your women's collection – which you've been showing since the end of 2010.

My women's collection does indeed often look rather masculine. For example, there might be a hand-tailored, double-breasted coat. There's nothing like that in my men's collection. But I have to say that my men's collection has become more masculine since I also started designing clothes for women.

But you wouldn't consider doing a unisex collection?

Never. I'm always interested in playing with the subject of man and woman, but I find unisex fashion dreadful. A man and a woman can't both wear the same jacket; their bodies are too different. A woman can wear a jacket that looks masculine, but it's still cut differently. And the other way around: there are jackets for men that are cut in a masculine way, but which look feminine. You can't just standardize them both. You always need the contrast – and a balance between the two.

At what point did you realize: Wow, my label is really taking off! Was it in 2009, when Hedi Slimane photographed Robert Pattinson in one of your outfits for AnOther Man? Or when Terry Richardson photographed a Damir Doma coat for Purple, in a fashion editorial styled by Carine Roitfeld?

To be honest, that sort of thing doesn't really interest me. Names don't mean anything. For me, all people are equally important – someone like Terry Richardson is no more

'Everyone can use fashion to express him or herself. Not everyone can sing, and not everyone can paint or dance. But everyone dresses.'

Looks from the autumn/winter 2012/13 men's collection (top and middle row) and from the spring/summer 2013 collection (bottom row)

Look from the spring/summer 2013 women's collection

Look from the spring/summer 2013 men's collection

Looks from the autumn/winter 2012/13 women's collection (top row and second row, left and centre) and from the spring/ summer 2013 collection (second row right)

important than any other photographer, and if *Vogue* writes something about me, I'm no more pleased than if some other publication runs an interview with me. Those are the values that I learned from my parents.

But you can't deny the fact that names are important for the success of your labels. You don't do conventional advertising. So if Robert Pattinson, Lenny Kravitz or Kanye West wear your designs in public, it makes you more visible ...

Of course. Nowadays pop stars and celebrities have enormous importance. It's all part of the new media culture, the internet, blogs, and so on. So if Lenny Kravitz or Robyn – whom I really like as a person – wear my clothes to the right event, that will bring me more publicity than my own fashion shows. That's great on the one hand, but on the other it's also sometimes hard for me to accept as a designer – because of course I personally am much more interested in my own fashion shows!

_Right at the beginning of your career, you found yourself a powerful finan-
cial partner: the German businessman Stephan Wembacher of the Paper Rain
Group. He believed in your potential as a designer – although he had no previous
experience in the fashion sector._

It is indeed very unusual for a young designer to find a partner who's prepared to over-
come certain business hurdles and to work consistently at something without allowing
himself to be distracted. But that's the only way it can work.

How exactly did his decision to join you come about?

That was during my first collection. While I was designing it, I developed my first business plan together with a friend who was working for an investment bank at the time. In
retrospect it was all very naive. I realized quite quickly that before long I would exhaust
my own resources. So I started speaking to business people. I wasn't particularly looking
for someone who had experience in fashion, but rather for someone who understood
what I was aiming at. Stephan Wembacher was the first person I met – and we got on
immediately. The company that he runs with his partners is involved in production, but
in the computer sector rather than in fashion and textiles. It's a completely different
business. Today, there are several partners in the company, and each has his or her own
area of responsibility.

_And the group is called Paper Rain – because of the money that just comes pour-
ing in?_

That would be nice! No, money doesn't come pouring into our company either.
As I said at the beginning, it's hard work. It all has to be run professionally. But
what my partners love about it – as I do – is the way we're building up a brand. It's
one thing to design an opening collection as I did in my first season. Then it really
was only about one specific silhouette, this one shirt and this one pair of trousers.
Nowadays I see everything more in global terms – it's a matter of building an entire
world.

_A world that apparently even has its own Damir Doma language: each of your
products has its own name; they're called Sayan, Pelly or Tarz._

In my very first collection the names actually had a meaning. All the products were
named after places where ghosts had been sighted. At that stage I could allow myself
to take the time to come up with names, but now there are far too many products
each season so it's no longer possible. Now the names are produced according to a
system.

What kind of system?

The names of the jackets all begin with the letter J, shirts begin with S, pants with P, and
so on. Also, we have a numerical system for the colours: 99 is black and 01 is white, and
the various colours lie between the two.

_So you haven't yet programmed your own Damir Doma name generator soft-
ware?_

Well, that would be interesting! No, that's the job of our interns. It's always one of the
first tasks we give them: come up with names. One intern once played a joke: our shoes
always begin with the letter F – F for footwear – and the intern's name was Froll. So the
shoe was called _Frolli_ …

Viviane SASSEN

FASHION PHOTOGRAPHER

Amsterdam

Art and fashion photography: Viviane Sassen has reached success in both fields, even as she blurs the boundaries between them – something perhaps attributable to Sassen's 'love-hate relationship' with fashion, as she puts it. Born in Amsterdam in 1972, Sassen studied fashion design and photography, receiving a Master of Fine Arts degree in Arnheim in 1997. Around the same time, she began shooting fashion stories for magazines (*AnOther, Numéro,* among others). *In and Out of Fashion*, a collection of Sassen's best fashion photos (Prestel, 2012), won the Kees Scherer Prize for the best Dutch photography book of 2011/2012. Most recently, her campaigns for the Parisian fashion house Carven attracted considerable attention, and her art photo series *Flamboya* and *Parasomnia*, compiled in East Africa between 2000 and 2011, were exhibited at the 2013 Venice Biennale.

Viviane Sassen, you grew up in Kenya between the age of three and five. Are your first memories of Africa?

Yes, my very first memories are of living in Kenya. My parents moved there because my father was a doctor and he worked there in a small village. I still have very vivid memories from that time.

Are your first fashion-related memories also from that time?

Well, I guess I wouldn't call them fashion memories. I remember seeing women with very colourful clothes, with different kinds of patterns. But I was much too young at the time to realize that this was something called fashion, and I didn't know yet that these clothes are a way for the women to express themselves. You know, the kangas and kitenges that women in East Africa wear, some of them have texts on them, and some have specific kinds of patterns and drawings that have a meaning.

Most people in the Western world take these strongly coloured, big-patterned wax fabrics to be 'traditional' African clothing, while actually they were popularized via Indonesia and the Netherlands in the 19th century.

Correct. They came to Africa via the Dutch textile manufacturer Vlisco. The company is still very well known in Africa.

In your photographic series *Flamboya* and *Parasomnia*, both shot in East Africa, you seem to subvert primitivist views of Africa. Your pictures often emphasize cultural exchanges between Africa and the Western world.

That's true. I like to play with different kinds of preconceived ideas about Africa, and I'd like to challenge the viewer to think about his or her own prejudices. But first of all, taking pictures in Africa is a very personal journey for me. It's not as if I want to express my own opinion about the continent. That would be ridiculous anyway. I mean Africa is huge. I'm aware that there's a sociological and political way to view my work, but most importantly, for me it's personal. My pictures are very much about ambiguity, and that's what I like about them.

One of the ambiguities lies in the fact that the photographs, taken in Kenya, Uganda, Tanzania and Ghana, fall somewhere between the categories of documentary photography and fashion photography. For example, one could wonder whether the people depicted in the pictures are actually wearing what they normally wear or whether they were styled by you?

Well, it depends. Normally people wear their own clothes. Sometimes we go to their closet and pick something together, but most of the time it's just what people are wearing at that moment. And sometimes I buy clothes at the local market: all second-hand stuff from Europe and the USA, such as the T-shirt worn by the boy in the picture *Paradise Lost*. I gave it to him and he put it on. I try to really collaborate with my models and get to a level where we can both bring ideas in. Sometimes it goes really fast, it can be a quick encounter, but then some other models I know for much longer. We meet and talk and I show them my sketches and my ideas, and we often stay in touch via email or Facebook.

Viviane Sassen, *Paradise Lost*, 2005

Often in your pictures – not only the ones from Africa, but also in your fashion work – the models don't look straight into the camera. Why is that?

First of all, for me this is a way to make images that are more abstract. As soon as you see a face, you know how to read the picture. But I like images that don't give themselves away too easily. When I do a series of pictures, or of one situation, I often find myself choosing the one picture where the face is not too visible. I think that's because I can look at it for a longer time. It's more exciting because you cannot grasp it at first glance. It's more universal.

So your pictures are about exposing the people they depict, but about respecting a certain distance at the same time?

Absolutely. And also there's an enormous range of possibilities to express emotion not through the face, but through the body. You know, you can express so much just by concentrating on body language, on a movement or the shape of the body. But if you see a face full-frontal, the picture is only about that particular person; you lose the universal aspect.

Maybe these pictures also correspond with modern culture in a broader sense? Since the advent of digital culture and surveillance cameras, a lot of people sense that it might be important not to be so recognizable, and think about guarding their own faces more. Because nowadays, with Google Glass and other technologies, you don't even know when your face is being recorded and exposed anymore.

You mean my photographs correspond with the signs of the time? Well, I've never thought about it this way. For me, again, it's much more personal. I did some modelling myself for a while when I was younger, and at that time I always thought of myself as a very shy exhibitionist. I also did a lot of self-portraits back then, a lot of nudes as well. So I'm quite familiar with this kind of exhibitionist feeling of showing your body, but then at the same time being shy and wanting to hide your face. This contradiction intrigues me.

How does this contradiction work out in the fashion context? Fashion campaigns tend to be all about showing beautiful faces. How hard is it to be allowed by your clients to not show the faces full-frontal?

Well, it depends on the client. If I work for a brand that is more conservative, I often do have the faces in the pictures, but then sometimes, with brands that are more open-minded, I can do different things. Don't get me wrong, I don't mind taking pictures of faces. It's not as if I *always* want to hide them.

Which brand allows you the most creative freedom for its campaigns?

Recently, working on the Carven campaigns has been really great. Guillaume Henry, the creative director of Carven, is very much interested in photography, he loves my work and he has been following it for quite some time. It's super interesting to work with him. For instance, we've done a campaign for the autumn/winter season 2013/14 in which many pictures are blurred, the girls and the clothes are out of focus. I think for a commercial fashion campaign that's quite daring.

Your spring/summer 2012 campaign for Carven was also quite remarkable. The models seemed to more or less crouch between game lines on a gymna-

Viviane Sassen for Carven, autumn/winter 2013/14

sium floor, and no matter how you turned the magazine, the ad somehow always seemed to be upside down – as if constantly being viewed from the wrong angle …

Yes, that campaign was very abstract. But you know, Carven is quite a flexible company. It doesn't belong to a big group, so that's how Guillaume Henry can get away with things like that. The Carven campaigns often happen very quickly. I feel the freedom to do what I think is good, and I throw ideas at Guillaume, and he will have ideas, too, and will throw them at me. So most of the time we send just one or two emails, have one talk on the phone, and then we decide which concept we want to go for.

Is it true that your career as a campaign photographer started in 2001 but was, in a way, cut short by 9/11? You shot a Miu Miu campaign for spring/summer 2002, but after that you didn't do any other campaigns for quite a while …

Yes, Miu Miu was the very first campaign I did, and it was completed shortly before 9/11. Pretty much everything changed after that. I remember that the people at Prada were actually very enthusiastic about my campaign, but after 9/11 everything became much more conservative and commercial. People got hesitant, I guess. Suddenly it was all back to Steven Meisel and Mario Testino and all those well-known people – you know, campaigns with lots of girls in the picture and as many bags and shoes as possible. I mean, how many products can one fit into a single picture?

In what way did your Miu Miu campaign differ from that maximalist approach?

Well, first of all, I think that choosing me as a photographer was daring in itself, because at that time I was still very young and didn't have a lot of experience. So the people at Prada didn't know exactly what would come out of it. Miuccia Prada is actually known for liking to work with young photographers and giving them a chance,

Viviane Sassen for Carven, spring/summer 2012

Viviane Sassen for Miu Miu, spring/summer 2002

which is great. But I had heard horror stories about people who had had to work on a campaign for three weeks in a row because she wasn't happy with the result, and who then had to reshoot over and over again. Luckily, she was very happy with what I did. They told me that I was the first photographer in years who had finished within the set time-frame.

The models in your Miu Miu campaign already assumed the kind of weird, sculptural body poses that you have come to be known for.

Well, I remember I came up with the idea of putting two girls in one picture, but with only the arms and legs of the second girl visible; you could not see her body or face. So, again, there was this kind of tension between being exposed and being hidden. I think it's these paradoxes and ambiguities that I just like to play with. And I've always been intrigued by weird body poses. You know, I've mentioned this in interviews before: when I lived in Kenya as a small kid, our house was next to the crippled children's home, where all the kids with polio were staying. They were my friends, and we would always play together in the playground. They had all these deformations of their arms and legs, and I found that very intriguing and really beautiful, and also very normal. I was too young to realize it was actually because of a terrible disease. I guess that's why there's this kind of sculptural element in the body poses that I love.

If one were to put it into a single sentence it would probably sound quite wrong: fashion photographer is inspired by polio ...

Oh, no! Of course it's not that simple and not as one-to-one. But anyway, when you're a kid and you experience everything for the first time, you're so open, you

Viviane Sassen, *DeLaMar Theater*, 2010

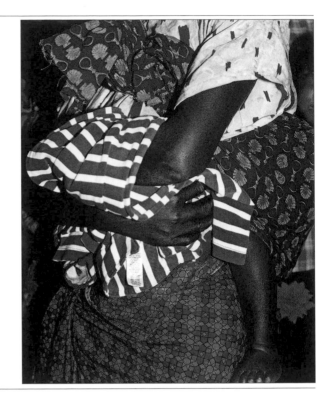

'Sometimes I do try to get a black model for a fashion campaign, but the brands usually tell me that it won't work for the Asian market.'

Viviane Sassen, *Mtoto*, 2006

don't have a judgement about things. The things we experience during those first childhood years are very important for the rest of our lives. They form a kind of blueprint.

So being familiar with different body shapes as a child created a certain longing for a broader variety of shapes than those usually represented in fashion photography?

Exactly. I guess it translates in this way.

Interestingly, the sculptural elements in your fashion pictures also seem to be a means of toning down or even conceptualizing the sexiness and seductiveness of some of your models' poses. Do you intend to subvert the impression of erotic availability?

Well, as a woman taking photographs of other women, I think there's a difference between the male gaze on women and the female gaze on women. At least that's what I hope. I would like my images to be a bit more layered and the eroticism to be more hidden, less exposed. I do like it when the pose in an image is not only beautiful or not only sexy, because I find that much too flat and not intriguing at all. For me, an image has to itch, somewhere, somehow – or even to be funny sometimes.

It's striking that while you photograph many people in Africa, there are hardly any black models in the fashion campaigns you shoot.

Viviane Sassen, *Now & Then/Gold Coast*, 2007

Well, I think that black skin is more beautiful than white skin and I just love to photograph it. Sometimes I do try to get a black model for a fashion campaign, but if it's an international brand, they usually tell me that it won't work for the Asian market. And then I don't know if this is really the case, or if this is just a reason they make up in order to mask their shame about refusing black models. I guess that, unfortunately, it's quite often the latter.

Bernhard *WILLHELM*

FASHION DESIGNER

Paris

Bernard Willhelm's hallmarks include garish, colourful collections, 'anti-reflective' and thick with humour. Born in the Swabian city of Ulm in 1972, he studied at Antwerp's Royal Academy of the Arts and, in 1999, made his debut in Paris, where he has lived and worked since 2002. Fans of Willhelm include pop stars like Björk and Santigold – Carrie Bradshaw donned his gold-mirrored ski goggles in *Sex and the City 2* (2010) – and Willhelm collaborates with several accessory labels, including Camper and Mykita. In 2009, he was appointed Professor of Fashion at the University of Applied Arts in Vienna, following in the footsteps of, among others of note, Raf Simons, Karl Lagerfeld and Veronique Branquinho.

His shoes and socks. For me, they are the basis of everything. Shoes and socks determine your stance, the way you touch the ground.

You yourself wear heavy mountain boots with Smiley laces.

They are from one of my winter collections.

It's summer now ...

So what?

What do you notice first when you look at a woman?

Also her posture. Basically you can read a woman's character just by looking at the way she stands there, for example whether she wears flat shoes or heels. But actually when I design I hardly think about gender, I think much more about patterns. We always put a lot of effort into our patterns, which are usually derived from abstract ideas. So it doesn't really matter whether our clothes end up being worn by men or women.

Then why do you even distinguish between women's and men's collections?

Sometimes I ask myself the same question. In Europe and America, this distinction is fixed deep in our minds. It's different in Japan, where our collections are most successful and where a large part of our garments is produced. If the Japanese like the look of something, they don't care so much which gender it was designed for. Japanese men buy women's clothes, and vice versa.

Coming back to body posture: you yourself seem to be pretty much of a fitness freak.

Well, if you don't have some kind of sense of body, you might as well forget becoming a designer. You do need to be able to perceive und understand your own body to work in this profession.

When do you have time for sport?

I don't have a television at my home. Other people lounge in front of the box or write email. I prefer to spend a couple of hours at the gym in the evening. That triggers endorphins. And what I also like about sport is that it gives me a certain power over my own body: I can mould what God has given me in whichever way I like.

Doping?

No. But I do keep an eye on what I eat. Food is important. However I do find doping interesting ...

What do you mean?

A few years ago I collaborated with François Sagat – he's a gay French porn star. He told me that in the porn scene, all men are addicted to anabolics. In pornography your body is the only thing that matters. François described it this way: taking anabolics is like being anorexic. Either you want more all the time, or all you want is less.

What do you as a fashion designer find interesting about pornography?

That sex looks so cloned today. I think it has to do with the Aids crisis. During the 1970s, before Aids, the people in porn films still had creative sex with pubic hair. This play-

François Sagat in a look from the spring/summer 2008 men's collection fitted to his physique

ful aspect has been lost as a result of Aids. Nowadays in porn it's all about the lighting. And fashion has changed radically since the advent of Aids. In the 1970s you already had men wearing short pants and very tight jeans – men who weren't gay. But since Aids, men's fashion has become very *sexless* again. All those baggy pants in the hip-hop scene …

But Hedi Slimane, while he was at Dior Homme in the early 2000s, popularized ultra-slim suits for men …

Well, first of all, Hedi Slimane didn't come up with these suits himself; he got the idea from Raf Simons, who had designed very similar suits years before, in Antwerp. And secondly, our collection with François Sagat was not simply about a slim line. We wanted our collection to be aggressively sexy: 'Show the cock, show the ass!' All the clothes were fitted to François' body. It might seem hard to believe, but actually he has a fashion background. He studied fashion design at the famous Studio Bercot, and he was Carine Roitfeld's personal assistant at French *Vogue*. I'm totally fascinated by him. His shaved head with the blue tattoo, these ultra-strong muscles … François has turned himself into an art object! We also did a calendar with him.

You often talk about 'we' …

By that I mean my business partner Jutta Kraus, with whom I started my label, and the whole team behind us. There are no lone geniuses in the fashion world, even if the press would like us to think that. Do people really believe that Karl Lagerfeld designs all of his collections himself? Of course he doesn't.

That reminds me of Fassbinder's *The Bitter Tears of Petra von Kant*. The film tells the story of an egocentric fashion designer who has a devoted slave who does all the work for her, including designing. Petra von Kant just lies in bed and chats on the phone all the time …

It is a great film! Of course Fassbinder says a great deal about the fashion business here. Producing a collection is always teamwork – but only the name of the designer gets mentioned. The people who work away hidden in the background don't get any share of the glamour that is supposed to abound in fashion. In that respect, *The Bitter Tears of Petra von Kant* is still very relevant today.

In 2007 you designed a sculpture for the cover of Björk's album *Volta*, which reminded of a fat bird, a Christmas cracker and a sarcophagus …

It's an exploding ball of energy with very large feet! Luigi Ontani's work inspired me to create it – he's an Italian artist who is known for his clay objects, including clay models of antipodes. In the ancient world, when people still believed that the Earth was flat, they thought that there were antipodes living on the opposite side of the

Sculpture for the cover of Björk's *Volta* album, shot by Nick Knight (2007)

Earth to keep the world in balance. Antipodes don't have a specific physical form – people imagined them to be balls that moved by rolling and that could change their shape.

Just like the shapeshifters in Star Trek?

More or less. Björk liked the clay sculptures by Ontani immediately and she thought they were very fitting for her album.

The Volta sculpture was also part of your retrospective Het Totaal Rappel at the ModeMuseum in Antwerp in 2008.

Yes, in 2006 my business partner Jutta and I donated our archive to the ModeMuseum. We didn't want to have our clothes hanging in our attic for another ten years, squashed up on clothes rails. You know, clothes go bad if they aren't stored properly; they have a sell-by date just like food. So we thought it was a good idea to hand them over to a museum, where they would be stored professionally and where something would still happen with them.

The title of the exhibition, Het Totaal Rappel …

That is the Belgian title of the Arnold Schwarzenegger film *Total Recall*. I love such pop references. But the translation is actually not quite correct: *Het Totaal Rappel* can also mean 'The Final Call'.

In the exhibition there was a Pepsi vending machine. Was that a pop reference, too?

Of course. Pepsi always makes me think of Michael Jackson and how his hair went up in flames when he filmed a Pepsi commercial in the 1980s.

The vending machine stood in the largest exhibition room, where it was the only exhibit. What was that all about?

I just loved the idea that we would use the most beautiful room of the museum to put in something very trivial. I couldn't stand placing the most important installation in the best room. I have something like an anti-reflex that makes me rebel against that sort of thing.

What do you mean?

Well, my mind is a bit more complicated. That's why, for example, I'm so fascinated with a label like Tommy Hilfiger. Basically, their whole business revolves around one single idea, which is to put the American flag on everything they sell – underwear, babywear or bed linen. Quite simple and straightforward. I could never even think like that!

How does your anti-reflex resonate with your licensing partners? Since 2008 you have a shoe line with Camper, and since 2009 there have also been Bernhard Willhelm sunglasses made by the Berlin-based Mykita label.

Well, with these collaborations we try to keep afloat as a small, independent label in the context of huge brands, like Hilfiger, who by now basically design their entire own universes. Unfortunately it is becoming increasingly difficult to survive in the fashion world. Nowadays a label could never survive by selling clothes alone; so accessory collaborations like these secure our existence.

Are you also interested in these collaborations because of the knowledge transfer that goes with them?

Of course. Sunglasses and shoes are products that a small label can hardly develop all on its own. Sneakers, for example, are a highly technical product requiring many different components. The sole of a sports shoe is not simply stamped out and cut like a leather sole; it has to be injection-moulded, poured, vulcanized and glued.

Is that why so many designers, when they add sneakers to their product range, use the standard sole of the running shoe of the Federal German Army or the Common Projects sole? Margiela, Marc Jacobs, Givenchy, Damir Doma, Balenciaga – they all use the same sole …

Yes. Designers often go with a sole that is already on the market, in order to reduce costs – and to get around developing their own sole.

With Camper you were able to develop your own, totally new zigzag sole.

Which initially turned out much too heavy. But it was improved from season to season. It took two or three years before it was perfect. In the beginning nobody knew whether the investment would ever pay off for Camper. The shoes were not an instant success, you know. It took a while before people really started buying them – and before even John Galliano wore them.

John Galliano?

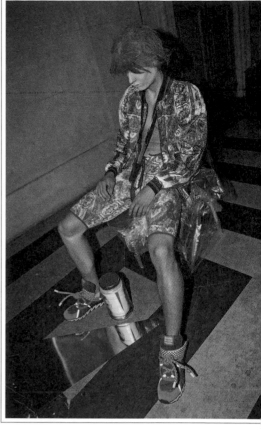

Look from the spring/summer 2013 men's collection with the zigzag-sole Camper trainers

Yes! In Paris the shoe was popular around the time when Galliano was fired from Dior. So when he had to appear in court for the hearing of his case, he wore my shoes. People might say that that was not necessarily the best PR for me – but I thought it was hilarious. Maybe that was my anti-reflex again? And then a bit later people in New York caught on and started wearing those shoes as well.

So the trend migrated?

Exactly. That is something I've learned through the licensing collaborations: that sometimes you have to keep on repeating certain products over and over again. Sometimes it's just not enough to produce a good design for one season only. Some things have to keep reappearing – until people recognize them and want to buy them. For a creative person like me it's maybe a bit boring to design the same shoe every season with just slight alterations, but well … every label needs its classics.

Franz, the gold-mirrored ski goggles from your collaboration with Mykita, are another of those classics. They became a big hit after Sex and the City 2.

Yes, when Sarah Jessica Parker wore *Franz* in the film in 2010, Mykita started selling 200

The *Franz* sunglasses from the Mykita collaboration

pairs per day. For Mykita these were fantastic sales – you know, their sunglasses are made in Germany and they are actually quite expensive!

Was Patricia Field, the stylist of *Sex and the City* and *The Devil Wears Prada*, personally responsible for putting *Franz* on Parker?

You mean whether I know Patricia Field personally? I don't. Patricia Field has an entire team of stylists working for her, and they collect huge numbers of clothes for each film, and of course they get sent all sorts of stuff by designers – because it's great advertising if a product appears in a film. So there's an entire warehouse stuffed with the latest products, and a huge table covered with sunglasses. I guess when they realized that Sarah Jessica Parker would be wearing a white dress in *Sex and the City* 2, there wasn't a very large selection of matching gold-mirrored sunglasses – *et voilà*!

Did you find that strange?

Not at all! That's the way things go in fashion. Lots of things happen by chance.

Which other collaborations could you imagine? Bernhard Willhelm watches with Swatch?

I'm not very interested in watches. But I was on the brink of signing a contract for sexy underwear. Unfortunately that didn't work out.

With Schiesser?

No, Schiesser is going bust anyway. But you know, in my early days – before I went to study fashion in Antwerp – I did my very first internship at Schiesser AG, in Radolfzell on Lake Constance. At the time there were still all sorts of Paloma Picasso licences, and Schiesser produced Paloma Picasso bedlinen, amongst other things. So during lunch break in Radolfzell people would gossip about things like: 'When you lie in bed at night in your Paloma Picasso bedlinen and dream of Paloma's hot red lips, would you want to wear matching Picasso pyjamas?' That's how I started out, really!

Have you ever thought about creating your own perfume? That's the way most fashion labels make their money.

I know, but launching a perfume only makes sense if you have a little advertising budget of 10 million euros. We haven't got 10 million.

Suppose you had: what would a Bernhard Willhelm perfume smell like?

Spicy! Cloves, nutmeg, cinnamon … But *Égoïste* by Chanel is such a good spicy scent already, it's impossible to beat. But maybe a perfume smelling of liquorice might be a new idea?

A liquorice perfume in a flacon that looks like your Björk sculpture would surely be a success. Like Jean Paul Gaultier's perfume in the Madonna bustier …

That isn't a Madonna bustier – that's just what people think. Gaultier copied that flacon one-to-one from *Shocking*, the perfume by Elsa Schiaparelli. She was the fantastic Surrealist fashion designer who worked in Paris at the same time as Coco Chanel. Today hardly anyone remembers her name. People have such short memories!

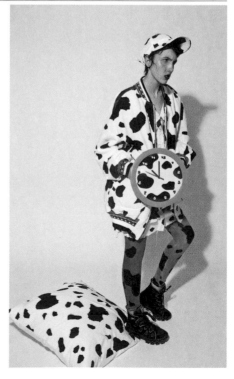

'I guess when they realized that Sarah Jessica Parker would be wearing a white dress, there wasn't a very large selection of matching gold-mirrored sun-glasses – et voilà!'

Looks from the autumn/winter 2013/14 women's collection

BLESS

FASHION AND PRODUCT DESIGNERS

Ines Kaag (Berlin) and Desiree Heiss (Paris)

For them, design is never an end in itself – it's precisely this 'strict' conceptual approach that enables German design duo Bless to produce captivating, and often amusing products again and again. Designers Desiree Heiss (born in Freiburg in 1971) and Ines Kaag (born in Fürth in 1970) formed Bless in 1997. Working between Paris and Berlin, Bless produces not only cunning casual clothing (motto: 'Fits every style!') but also vacuum-cleaner chairs, winter hammocks and jewellery for electrical cables. The two avid aikidokas have shared a professorship at the Staatliche Hochschule für Gestaltung Karlsruhe since 2006, and in 2013 were recruited as guest professors by the renowned Pratt Institute in New York.

Ines Kaag, Desiree Heiss, in an interview you once mentioned in disgust: 'Design rears its ugly head everywhere.' Do you still stand by this remark?

Ines Kaag: Absolutely. If you want to buy an iron today, you're in shock when you go to the household goods department and realize that all irons actually look like dolphins.

Desiree Heiss: Vacuum cleaners look like Smart cars, and ghetto blasters remind you of spaceships. All these products claim to be design objects, and yet they are mostly so ugly that when you take them home you immediately want to hide them. After using them, you put them right away. So they're classic examples of how design can go off on a completely wrong tangent, because it neither supports the function nor is it helpful in any way.

It seems unusual for fashion designers to take such a critical and pragmatic approach to design.

Kaag: Design for design's sake has never interested us. Even as fashion students we found it pointless. A product that's used by everyone doesn't need a particularly outlandish shape. And just because you want to be a fashion designer doesn't mean that you have to create collection after collection according to some new idea, simply because the popular notion of being a fashion designer is to let your creative fantasies run riot twice a year. We don't feel the desire to 'indulge' in colours or shapes or to come up with some sort of 'vision'.

So what is your guiding principle, then?

Kaag: Our starting point is actually quite matter-of-fact, very reduced. We ask ourselves simple questions, for example: What do we still need? What is missing in our wardrobes? Is there something that other designers have not done better yet? If you look at it this way, maybe what we do shouldn't even be considered fashion design. We're more concerned with finding constructive ways of dealing with problems and deficits.

Heiss: That's why, every season, we struggle to find an answer for those fashion journalists who want to know what the 'theme' of our new Bless collection is.

Kaag: We hate that question.

You launched Bless in the fashion context in 1997 with a fur hat that looked like Rod Stewart's hairdo. Martin Margiela liked it so much that he incorporated it into

his autumn/winter 1998 collection. Since then, you've refused to restrict yourselves to fashion and have always designed chairs, shopping bags and hotel
rooms as well.

Heiss: At that time, the fashion scene seemed very open; there was a real spirit of
change. It was the time when people like Helmut Lang and Martin Margiela became
successful – designers who consciously tried to change things in fashion and who refused to abide by the rules. And there was an entire generation of young designers
starting out at more or less the same time as we did – Viktor & Rolf, for example. The
fashion industry was looking for innovation. It was the right moment for us to come
up with a new concept. However, the very thing that made us special in the beginning –
the fact that besides fashion we also design shelves, CD covers, etc. – has now been
adopted. Today, you'll hardly find a fashion designer who doesn't also design furniture
and all sorts of other things – look at Hedi Slimane, for instance. That a designer has
good taste in music and releases his own compilation CD, like Karl Lagerfeld, or that
he takes an interest in art and builds up a collection – nowadays that, too, is kind of a
given.

Hedi Slimane and Karl Lagerfeld are designers who like to perform their personalities publicly. From the very beginning, you refused to do that with Bless. You
don't even give out photos of yourselves.

Kaag: We avoid stepping into the picture as individuals because our products already reflect our own needs very precisely. In this respect, our work is extremely personal. While
we are pleased to share that aspect of ourselves, we don't like to draw attention to our
faces. That would be too much.

You've mentioned in several interviews that you're both enthusiastic practition-
ers of the Japanese martial art aikido. To what extent is that important for your
work?

Heiss: Well, first of all, aikido is good exercise, of course.

Kaag: Aikido enables us to stay physically balanced so that we're able to work regularly
as long and persistently as we do – without losing the overall rhythm of our lives.

But what's the sport's significance beyond that? When you say that at Bless you
never design things randomly, that it always takes a reason, a problem that needs
solving, then that reminds me of the philosophy of aikido.

Kaag: That's true. Aikido is a defensive martial art based on the principle that you redir-
ect the energy of an attack that somebody is directing at you. You don't block the attack, but divert it and turn it against the attacker himself. You could indeed transfer this
philosophy to our design approach in many respects.

Meaning that it acts as a neutralizing factor?

Heiss: Exactly. Our vacuum-cleaner chair is a good example: it's a wooden chair into
which we integrated a hidden vacuum cleaner.

Kaag: When you look at the chair, you might think that it's actually a compromise
turned product – maybe I really wanted to create a vacuum cleaner while Desiree preferred the idea of a chair, so we settled on a vacuum-cleaner chair. But that's not the
way it was.

Heiss: Our aim was to neutralize the vacuum cleaner, so to speak, within the chair.

'Instead
of designing
something new,
we would often
prefer to delete
some other
product that
is already
available.'

Looks from the *N°48 Presuture*
series (2013)

Kaag: This product was created as part of our series *Design Relativators*. The idea behind it was that, instead of creating a collection of new products, we would basically do the opposite and not design anything. Because, to be honest, instead of designing something new, we would often prefer to delete some other product that's already available. You know, get rid of something ugly, unnecessary, annoying.

Minus-design, so to speak?

Heiss: If you like. Our mixer was a similar product: it consisted of an electric drill and a whisk. We wanted to make clear that you could easily make certain products disappear by combining them with products that have similar functions – such as using an electric drill to mix a cake.

And that, too, could be linked to the philosophy of aikido?

Heiss: It would be unfair to say that aikido is the formula for everything we do. There are some Bless products that don't have anything to do with that.

For example, when you design a pair of jeans although there are really plenty of jeans already?

Kaag: When we design a pair of jeans, our aim is not to establish our own jeans on the vast denim market. What prompted us to design our jeans was, once again, a problem: that there's a particular place in the front of most jeans where the belt always keeps slipping out. We find that annoying. So we designed a pair where the belt loop is pushed

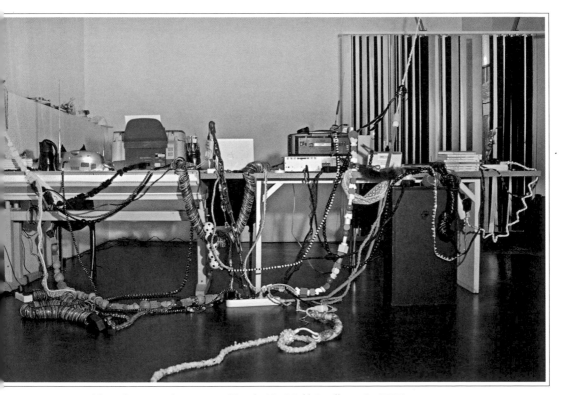

Adorned power and computer cables: the *N°26 Cable Jewellery* series (2005)

Clothes and accessories from the *N°28 Climate Confusion Assistance* series (2006);
in the back: wallpaper from the *N°29 Wallscapes* series (2006)

slightly to one side so that it can hold the belt better. It may seem a trivial thing to do, and we aren't doing anything spectacular here, but it is nonetheless a reaction to a nuisance.

And what about your Cable Jewellery? At first sight, this product doesn't seem to be about neutralizing a problem, but about the very opposite: making it prettier by ornamenting it. Cable Jewellery decorates power and computer cables with beads, fringes and small wooden blocks.

Heiss: Most people find power and computer cables lying round in rooms visually disruptive, but any attempt to make them disappear usually makes everything even worse. The plastic conduits and cable ducts that are installed so that the cables can be shoved inside them always look dreadful. Basically, they're the perfect anti-solution. So in the case of our *Cable Jewellery*, instead of trying to hide the cables, we found it interesting to emphasize them and turn them into decorative elements.

Kaag: Basically it's a very simple idea but therefore all the more amazing. When we presented the *Cable Jewellery*, a lot of people said: 'Yes! Finally someone has thought of it!'

Do you find it a paradox that products like Cable Jewellery or your Fur Hammock – a hammock lined with fur – didn't become sales hits because of their rather high prices, but that you're regularly invited to exhibit them in design shows and retrospectives?

Kaag: It is indeed basically a contradiction to exhibit our products in museums or galleries. They're really designed to be used – we don't consider them to be art objects. We are, however, always pleased to receive such requests.

How do you deal with them?

Kaag: When we receive invitations like that, our pragmatic solution is mostly to open up a temporary Bless shop in the exhibition. There, people can purchase our products while the show is running. It has worked very well. Once, in the case of our major Bless retrospective in the Museum Boijmans Van Beuningen in Rotterdam, we took a different approach. There, we decided to deal with the contradiction in another manner – by developing a new product especially for the exhibition: our *Wallscapes*. We photographed Bless products in the homes of people who have already bought a lot of our products. We then took these photographs and turned them into posters and wallpaper, which we hung in the museum at a scale of 1:1. This enabled visitors to the exhibition to visit the homes of various people virtually and look at the contexts in which Bless products are normally used.

So the idea was to make the visitor immediately think: Here I am in the museum, which is actually the wrong context?

Heiss: That was precisely our idea.

Earlier in the conversation, you spoke of the openness of the fashion world in the 1990s. Today, that seems to be over: innovators like Helmut Lang and Martin Margiela have quit, and the fashion business has become tougher. How do you react to these changes?

Heiss: Well, since Bless was never really part of the fashion world – operating in a sort of perpetual transit between different areas of life that are affected by fashion – our economic position has always been quite uncomfortable. You need to be able to withstand all weathers and enjoy testing your own strength. On the one hand it's true to say that the fashion business has become more conservative and commercial, but on the other hand it's fascinating to see what, for example, the internet has made possible: newcomers like Tavi Gevinson can join in at the highest level without having passed through the usual course. In that respect, every era has its advantages and disadvantages. We continue to see it as our task to make ourselves and the world better with products that cheer up our daily lives and force us to rethink things or see them in a different light.

You also seem to be interested in redefining the relationship between designer and customer: your continuing series *Contemporary Remediation* doesn't consist of one collection, but of an appeal to send in requests for products – which you might then fulfil in the next season.

Heiss: Usually, designers make suggestions for products and then wait to see whether they win approval or fizzle out unnoticed. With our appeal, we try to get away from this idea. We're interested in the art of abandoning, of listening and paying attention – in other words, abandoning the mediocrity that usually prevails, keeping our ears open as to whether there might be a general desire for change, and listening to find out exactly what people perhaps need and want. The objects produced in this series to date are characterized by the fact that they were sold out immediately.

Kaag: You could say the idea is to restructure our approach to supply and demand. The people who hand in requests are named in the product title, clearly communicating whose idea we've taken up. It's an experiment – one that's also prompted by the absurd phenomenon that the global fashion trade usually revolves around the fetish of exclusivity.

So how exactly does it work?

Kaag: We promise the customer whose idea formed the basis for a product that he or she will enjoy absolute exclusivity for one season, with the exception of our shops in Berlin and Paris. Should the product be successful there, we'll then include it at least temporarily in our line of so-called *Classics*, which is generally available. The product doesn't have to be anything totally new: sometimes people request the reissue of an older Bless product, for example in a material that's specific to them. So *Contemporary Remediation* is a sort of service in which we can apply our experience in the field of production alongside our aesthetic preferences. For us, it's a logical reaction to the capricious nature and diversity – you could also say the interchangeability – of today's potpourri of fashion.

Have you ever received a particularly attractive customer request that you would have liked to fulfil but had to turn down?

Heiss: We haven't really succeeded in developing pyjamas that you would wear outside to go to the bakery in the morning. And so far, we've also failed to create a bag that doesn't cost anything. But we haven't given up on either project!

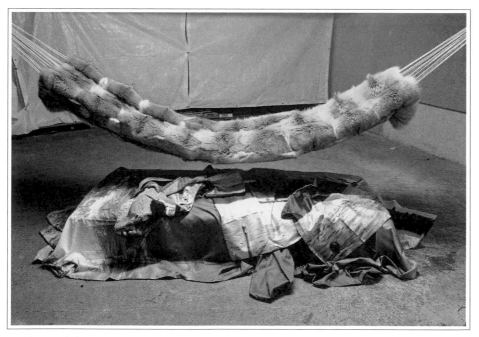

Fur hammock from the *N°28 Climate Confusion Assistance* series (2006) and bedsheets with digital lake print from the *Bless Classics* series

Miguel ADROVER

FASHION DESIGNER

Majorca

Miguel Adrover is the favourite agent provocateur of the contemporary fashion world – a designer whose outspoken pronouncements are as loved as they are hated. Born on the Spanish island of Majorca in 1965, Adrover is equally critical of both the increasingly rapid acceleration of collection cycles and the industry's lack of environmental awareness. A close friend of Alexander McQueen's, his own label collapsed early in the new millennium after he was accused of sympathizing with Islamism. Adrover then went on to design collections for a German eco fashion label. Although his comeback show, presented under his own name in New York in 2012, was highly acclaimed by critics, Adrover was unable to find a new investor – nor was he offered a position with another fashion house. Could it be that Adrover should learn how to keep his mouth shut?

Señor Adrover, you seem to think that there's a lot wrong with fashion today.
Almost everything's wrong! Fashion today is all about powerful conglomerates and their marketing divisions trying to sell us nothing but hot air and illusions at ridiculous prices. Instead of focusing on creativity, the multinationals focus only on squeezing their customers' brains and emptying their pockets. I mean, fashion used to be about freedom, right? What happened to that? Is everybody really free today to wear exactly what they want? Of course not. Fashion is just overly following trends.

But trends are an important part of what constitutes fashion.
Well, but they used to come from the underground. They were born by an avant-garde of artists and musicians. Today, trends are ready-made by the industry, designed at the drawing desks of the conglomerates that spend billions on advertising to push their products on the market. And celebrities like Ronaldo, David Beckham and Lady Gaga help them at it.

You're said to like to rail against Karl Lagerfeld especially.
When I say I hate him, I don't mean it in a personal way. I just think that at his age he should start to move over and clear the way for a younger generation and a new philosophy in fashion. I don't believe in what he stands for as a designer. Take Chanel, for example: of course Coco Chanel was a very important designer. Her costumes were helpful in liberating women striving for emancipation. In designing these costumes, Chanel helped to change society. But what does Chanel stand for today under Lagerfeld? Nothing but a bloated myth! Brainwashing! It's similar with all the big houses that have dominated fashion for decades: Dior, Yves Saint Laurent – their philosophies are just as antiquated as their houses.

So you long for young talent and fresh names in fashion?
Absolutely. But it has become very difficult to start your own house as a young designer. Look at Nicolas Ghesquière: everybody says that he's the best fashion designer in the world. But instead of using his talent to launch his own label and promote his name, he was kept in a gilded cage for years by the Gucci group at Balenciaga. I think it's a very frustrating situation today. Young people hardly succeed in getting their statements across – but more and more of them want to work in fashion. They just keep pouring out of fashion schools. Where will they all end up? If they're lucky, they may manage to grab a job in one of the conglomerates and design one of the cruise, resort or Christmas collections that flood the market. Poor things! When I left Majorca in 1991, there was only one fashion school. Today they have nine fashion schools on Majorca – an island with only 900,000 inhabitants. Almost every village has its own Fashion Week. I mean, how are we going to end up!?

What you propose is to slow down fashion and put the emphasis back on quality. But if you watch documentaries on haute couture ateliers in Paris, for example at Chanel, you see exactly that: highly specialized craftsmanship, complicated custom-making, quality at a high price that is likely to prevent the clothes from being thrown away after only one season. What's bad about that ...?

First of all, people who can afford haute couture have so much money, they don't even realize that the clothes are actually expensive. Secondly, if a company runs a haute couture department today with 30 women sewing a single dress for weeks, that only means that this company has lots of power and financial resources. The money needed to maintain doing haute couture doesn't come from selling couture, of course. The ateliers are subsidized by the profits made from prêt-à-porter, perfume and underwear licences, all the cheap merchandise. Haute couture is only an image division serving to increase the prestige of a luxury company.

If everything is so horrible – why do you still work in fashion?

It's simple: you cannot change a system from outside. To be able to affect fashion, you need to be part of the system. You need to hate it and try to change it constantly. That's how my close friend Alexander McQueen did it. His creativity was violent; he introduced a whole new vocabulary into fashion and he managed to build his own brand. Not very profitable – but new!

But even McQueen went into partnership with the Gucci group in late 2000.

Unfortunately, yes. After signing his contract with them things changed quickly. The pressure was on, so to speak – which did not necessarily make him a happier man, you know.

How did you meet McQueen?

In London. A friend from my village on Majorca did an internship at his studio. I went to visit my friend and we went for dinner, and there I met Lee – that's what his friends called him. We got along very well. At the time, I was living in New York, but I spent my summer holidays on Majorca. Sometimes Lee would come to visit me there. He was often broke, just like me. We both have simple backgrounds, you know: I come from a family of almond farmers, Lee's father was a cab driver, and he grew up in a council flat. I remember Lee was with me on Majorca when he got his contract at Givenchy, starting as creative director there. That was in 1996. At the time, he had shown only a few of his own collections in London. He got the call from LVMH – and suddenly the money started pouring in!

You worked for McQueen for a while – before you started your own label.

Yes, I was consulting for Lee. I flew to London frequently to help him out; I brought materials and accessories. For example, I gave him the antelope horns that he used in his *It's a Jungle Out There* collection in 1997. Usually I would spend three or four weeks with him during the preparations for his next show. And whenever Lee was in New York, he would stay at the Four Seasons Hotel, but he spent most of his time with me in my tiny basement apartment. I remember when Anna Wintour's assistant came to get Lee for meetings with American *Vogue*, he had to virtually kick at my door hard to get Lee out.

When you started your own label in 1999, you worked with found materials. For example, you used an old Burberry coat or the fabric of a discarded mattress, or you customized a Louis Vuitton bag and turned it into a miniskirt. Were these already ecological statements?

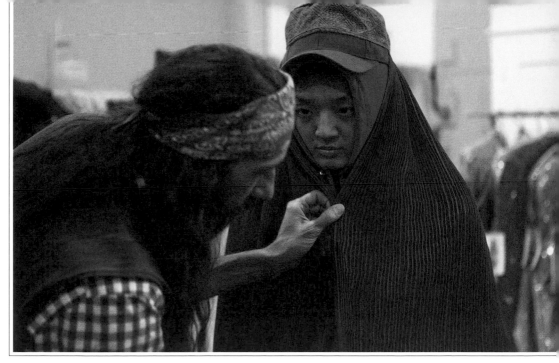

Backstage at the *Out of My Mind* show in New York in February 2012: Miguel Adrover putting the finishing touches to a look

Not really. That came from financial necessity more than anything. I had no money to buy fabrics, so I went and collected them from the trash. I knew about certain factories that often put good stuff in their garbage. If you know New York well enough, you really can find anything there for free!

Even Louis Vuitton bags?

No, the bag was given to me by someone, as a donation, so to speak. But the mattress I really did find on the street.

Allegedly it belonged to Quentin Crisp, the legendary eccentric to whom Sting dedicated his song 'Englishman in New York'.

That's right. Quentin Crisp was my neighbour, he lived in the basement apartment next door to mine. Sometimes I would run into him at the diner around the corner and we would have breakfast together. A very nice old Brit! I know he had the reputation of being a flamboyant dandy, but he didn't seem pretentious to me at all. His apartment was just as small as mine, and he prided himself on not having cleaned it once in more than 20 years.

Quentin Crisp thought that dusting was unworthy of intellectual life, and he's legendary for his observation that dust layers stop growing after four years.

Well, you can imagine how seedy his mattress was! When Quentin died in the winter of 1999, the landlords cleaned out his apartment within three days, throwing his stuff out on the street – they wanted a new tenant in as quickly as possible. So I found the mattress on the sidewalk one night, all covered in snow, and I dragged it into my apartment with a friend. We both developed rashes right away, that's how dirty it was! But I really liked its fabric – this bluish beige, striped fabric that you find on mattresses in the United States. I cut a skirt and coat from it, without washing the fabric or anything; today the outfit is part of the Costume Collection of the Metropolitan Museum's Fashion Institute!

At the time, your clothes were featured in photo shoots in American *Vogue* and critics like Suzy Menkes were full of praise for you. But your rise ended abruptly in September 2001 after you presented your *Utopia* collection – two days before the attacks on the World Trade Center. The collection was perceived as being sympathetic towards Islam.

Yes, the media made it look like I had dressed my models as Taliban fighters, but that was not my intention at all. The *Utopia* collection was actually about bridging different cultures and saying: everybody live together peacefully! There was a strong Arab sense in the collection, that's true – it had been there already in my previous collection, *Meeteast*, in February 2001. But there were also a lot of influences from Peru, from different parts of Africa, from Majorca, and so on in the collection, hence its name: *Utopia*. It had nothing to do with sympathy for the Taliban! But of course it was easy for a lot of journalists to focus on the turbans and the long robes.

A combination that is certainly not worn by only the Taliban ...

Exactly, but right after 9/11 there seemed to be no way for nuanced reflections. To this day I don't mind admitting that I'm fascinated by the way the Taliban dress. Aesthetically, I find the silhouettes and patterns of their robes more interesting than a lot of the clothes we wear in the Occident. That doesn't mean I support terrorism! But, you know, over time, I've come to accept what happened to me back then. The negative press was proof that my fashion was not coming from a vacuum, but that it was actually committed to reality.

Your investor backed down, and you stopped designing under your own name in 2004. Between 2007 and 2012, you worked as creative director for hessnatur, a German eco fashion brand. Fashion and sustainability – aren't these actually polar opposites?

You mean because fashion creates a longing for products that you don't really need? No, I don't see it that way. What's important is that the materials used are grown organically and that social standards are respected on the production side.

But why does eco fashion in most cases look so ... ecological?

That's a problem, indeed. Organic fabrics and materials should be used for more radical fashion – to attract younger and edgier customers. These clothes would have wooden buttons instead of plastic ones, and the thread would be cotton, not nylon; but apart from that the process of constructing the garment would be exactly the same. There is no reason why eco fashion should be less strong visually than other clothes. At hessnatur I was working on that and we were actually on the right track. But there's still a way to go.

So the reason that there is hardly any eco fashion available in, let's say 'shocking pink', is not that this colour cannot be dyed in an eco-friendly way?

Maybe it's not possible to reproduce every single chemical dye organically, but most of them you can, no problem. Natural dyes really don't have to look boring; there's more than just muddy earth tones. Just think of paella! Saffron and bell pepper powder can

One of the dresses patched together by hand from the *Out of My Mind* show in February 2012

'People in the industry say I'm toxic. I don't understand that. I'm toxic because I have social awareness? That's bad? I don't think so!'

Fur hat and carved wooden caps from the
Out of My Mind collection, 2012

be used for more than just dyeing rice – they're good for dyeing clothes as well, and they won't wash out!

In terms of social awareness, the success of American Apparel in recent years seemed to indicate that young costumers value the 'sweatshop-free' production of their clothes.

But American Apparel doesn't use only organic cotton. And besides, the company has grown so quickly, they basically exploded, so now they don't really know how to follow up with new products. They seem already on the verge of bankruptcy. That doesn't have much to do with sustainability.

Sometimes the key phrases 'sweatshop-free' and 'locally produced' seem to also trigger a strange knee-jerk nationalism. A lot of people consider T-shirts produced in Los Angeles to be better per se than T-shirts from China. And hessnatur – reacting to comments left by irritated costumers in their website's Q&A section – explain at length why they keep on purchasing fabrics from China.

China is the only country in the world where you can order organically dyed organic silk. This is Chinese know-how. So why not collaborate with the manufacturers there? Should the silk be shipped to some other place first to have it dyed there? That would be ridiculous. As I said earlier: it's important to have good conditions in factories and to pay the workers a fair wage. It's right to disapprove of sweatshops, but it would be totally wrong to say: from now on we'll have everything produced only at our very own doorstep. We must support local projects worldwide. For example, hessnatur collaborates with farmers in the high plains of Peru, who produce alpaca wool while making sure that their animals don't come in contact with pesticides or fertilizers. A lot of big fashion companies don't see why such small, direct measures are necessary. They just order their fabrics at the big fabric fair in Paris, without caring where the fabrics actually come from. The fashion industry thinks it's enough to start a charity campaign every now and then. But that's just marketing.

You mean Louis Vuitton ads with Angelina Jolie in Cambodia?

For example. What is Angelina Jolie doing in the Cambodian jungle with her Vuitton bag? Even Bono is doing ads for Vuitton! In the picture, you see him stepping out of a private plane in some African grassland with his wife. Why do they fly to Africa, wearing their diamond rings, while each day thousands of child workers die in African diamond mines? That's out of control!

In February 2012 you celebrated your return to New York Fashion Week with a new collection under your own name, the first in almost ten years. Entitled *Out of My Mind*, there were a striking number of middle fingers given in the collection: middle fingers attached to hats, middle fingers on shoes …

The middle fingers weren't meant as a message to New York, if that's what you think. Even after what happened to me there after 9/11, I still love fucking New York – and you can take that sentence both ways. The middle fingers were actually meant as a message to the fashion industry. Basically I was saying: 'Fuck you! You can do everything with nothing.' I made all the clothes in the show from items from my personal wardrobe. I repurposed them, not even using a sewing machine. Everything was hand-sewn.

The show received a huge amount of positive coverage. It seemed as if the fashion press wanted to finally make amends to you. For example, Cathy Horyn wrote in *The New York Times*: 'It's a pleasure to see someone do a lot with a little' – while trashing Alexander Wang's show in that very same review.

Well, thank you, Cathy Horyn! And who got the job as new creative director at Balenciaga? Not me! Sometimes I think it's a mistake to speak my mind. Maybe criticizing the fashion industry keeps me from getting offered jobs at high fashion labels?

Maybe it's more that the industry doesn't see how your ideas could be made profitable? In the same review, Cathy Horyn added: 'There is no business model here and he doesn't care.'

That isn't true. Of course I care about business. I've shown that I can work for other companies. I've worked successfully at hessnatur. And I wouldn't have any problem with being the designer for Yves Saint Laurent or Balenciaga – as long as the companies agreed to, you know, sustainability and so on. I'm open to working for anybody, really. But I hear that people in the industry say I'm toxic. I don't understand how I can be toxic when I do collections from recycled clothes and organic material. I'm toxic because I have social awareness? That's bad? I don't think so!

Valerie STEELE

FASHION HISTORIAN
New York

She is known in the United States simply as the 'Fashion Professor' (*Forbes*) or 'the high-heeled historian' (*New York Times*). Born in 1955, Valerie Fahnestock Steele is one of today's most prominent fashion historians and curators. After completing her studies in history, she received a doctoral degree from Yale in 1983 with a dissertation on fashion and eroticism in the Victorian Age. She has published books on fetish outfits and the gothic style. In 1997, Steele founded the academic journal *Fashion Theory: The Journal of Dress, Body & Culture,* where she remains editor-in-chief today. Since 2003, Steele has presented a number of exhibitions as director of the Museum at the Fashion Institute of Technology in New York. Her 2011 exhibition devoted to the haute couture wardrobe of Daphne Guinness was widely acclaimed.

Miss Steele, you're a historian by training. How did you choose fashion as your subject?

That was in my first year in graduate school at Yale University. I had come there in the late 1970s to work on a doctorate in modern European cultural and intellectual history. One assignment in class was to present a brief lecture on two scholarly articles and a classmate presented two from the feminist journal *Signs* on the Victorian corset. One was a traditional interpretation of the corset as being oppressive to women and dangerous, the other was revisionist, saying that the corset was sexually liberating. As soon as I heard that a light bulb went on and I realized: fashion is part of culture, I could do fashion history! I rushed to the library, but it quickly became evident that there were hardly any books on the subject. What you had mostly at the time was fashion journalism and a kind of antiquarian costume studies, but not a cultural and intellectual history of fashion. So I wrote my dissertation on fashion and eroticism during the Victorian era. My professors thought this was a very stupid idea.

Fashion was not taken seriously as a scholarly field yet?

Not at all! I remember at one point I was at a cocktail party for graduate students and a very famous historian of European intellectual history asked me what I was working on. So I said: 'Fashion.' And he said: 'Oh, that's fascinating – German or Italian?' I was dumbfounded, but then all of a sudden the penny dropped and I said: 'No, no, fashion like Paris, not fascism.' He just said 'oh,' turned around and walked away.

Like the corset, high heels have been a recurrent subject of debate within feminist critique. Could you explain their history and psychology?

High heels have existed throughout Western Europe since at least the 17th century. Prior to that you had some kind of platform shoe, but the technology of making a heel really became consistent then. High heels were at first worn by men as much as by women; they were an aristocratic phenomenon. There is, for example, Hyacinthe Rigaud's famous portrait of Louis XIV, the French Sun King, wearing high-heeled shoes and you can see the red heel and his calves in elegant silk stockings. But by the middle of the 18th century the high heel became increasingly associated with women's shoes. At that time you also had someone like Nicolas Edmonde Rétif de la Bretonne, the first

'Daphne Guinness told me that Manolo Blahnik always asks her: "Daphne, why do you wear those ugly shoes?"'

Shoe display at the *Daphne Guinness* show at the Museum at the Fashion Institute of Technology (2011); centre: Noritaka Tatehana; top and bottom: Nina Ricci

sort of recognized shoe fetishist who ran around Paris stealing women's shoes, kissing them and so on.

So Christian Louboutin's wildy popular high heels, with their red soles, could historically be traced back to the aristocracy of the 17th century?

Absolutely. You know, the Irish writer Sir Richard Steele, who my grandfather used to claim was an ancestor of ours, was the co-founder of *The Spectator* and he wrote that at one point in history women preferred a man with red heels and a fine waistcoat to someone with a sincere heart – in other words: women preferred a man who was an aristocrat and wealthy. But of course, by the time Louboutin was putting red soles on, red had switched from a colour that symbolized martial prowess and aristocracy to being a colour primarily associated with erotic sexual passion. So not only have men stopped wearing high heels, the symbolism of red has changed as well.

Why don't men wear heels anymore?

Well, you still have heels on men's boots occasionally, but only if they're practical – for example riding boots have heels that help you to stay in the stirrup. In the 19th century the focus in menswear shifted on practicability during the so-called *Great Masculine Renunciation*, which was connected with the emancipation of the middle classes. Men of the middle classes rejected the style of the aristocracy. So an 18th-century man could still wear a pink silk suit embroidered with flowers with lace cuffs and red heels, without anybody saying that he looked unmanly, but after the *Great Masculine Renunciation* such outfits were deemed effeminate. Heels became a prime symbol of female sexual beauty. And history shows that once something has been leached out of menswear and taken over by women, men almost never go back to it. It's as if it becomes contaminated. Basically, the only female accessory men have managed to grab back for themselves partly are earrings – which is kind of amusing because it looks as if they got in touch with their inner pirate again after the 19th century …

What do you make of the recent trends in high heels? Heels have become higher and higher, but there are also high-heeled platform shoes that don't have a stiletto. Their heel seems to magically hover up in mid-air.

Yes, you mean the shoes that Daphne Guinness or Lady Gaga wear. Amazing designs! There has in fact been a lot of experimentation with heels in recent years. I guess you could call these 'heel-less high heels'. Walking in them looks kind of dangerous, but they're surprisingly easygoing. The greatest creator of those is the Japanese designer Noritaka Tatehana, but Rick Owens and Alexander McQueen make similar ones.

Where do these heels originate from?

I don't know who made the first heel-less high heel. I have not been able to identify a clear history of that. They are really something new. At least they are not a part of the fetish lexicon where all you have is a subcategory of fetish imagery for fake ballet shoes in which you walk *en pointe* like a ballerina.

Heel-less high heels are not delicate and ballet-like at all, but chunky. They look like hoofs.

Yes, there is something grotesque and terrifying about them.

The *Dandyism* section at the *Daphne Guinness* show with outfits by Chanel, Alexander McQueen, Dior and Christian Lacroix

The *Exoticism* section at the *Daphne Guinness* show; right: evening coat by Rick Owens worn back to front over a sequined coat designed by Guinness herself

So in a way they invert the eroticism of the classic, more svelte high heel?

Absolutely. In a way they are the opposite of sexy shoes. A lot of the iconography that makes a stiletto the popular kind of sexy shoe is missing. That's why a lot of men hate them. Manolo Blahnik hates them. Daphne Guinness told me that Blahnik always asks her: 'Daphne, why do you wear those ugly shoes?' But fashion is interesting to women often not because it's trying to be sexy in a conventional way, but because it's new. These shoes are a transformation of design, an advancement of contemporary fashion. And designers who champion them, like Rick Owens or Alexander McQueen and his successor, Sarah Burton, have been willing to push aside the rules of what's beautiful and pursue looks that are transgressive in a way.

In 2011 the Fashion Institute of Technology honoured Daphne Guiness with an exhibition in which you displayed more than 100 pieces from her personal haute couture collection. In an interview, you have described Guinness as a 'fashion person's fashion person' – like an artist's artist?

Exactly. I think that for the average person, Daphne is kind of an enigma. Most people on the street will look at her and go: 'Oh my God, what is she doing?' Whereas for people in the fashion world, I mean people like Tom Ford and Valentino and a lot of photographers, she is a fashion goddess – because she is so fearless about what she wears. She is really an individualist with distinct and inspiring personal style in a field that is discouragingly full of lemmings who all look alike.

Is this what makes her so interesting? For several years now, she has been all over the fashion magazines.

When I spoke to Suzy Menkes from the *International Herald Tribune* she had an interesting idea as to why Daphne emerged so much into the media in the last few years. She feels that it has partly to do with the fact that the press only has room in its collective mind for one of what it calls an 'eccentric fashion icon'. This position was long held by Isabella Blow …

… who was Alexander McQueen's patron.

Right. And after Blow took her own life in 2007 the mantle fell on Daphne, so to speak. Since then, the media focus on her.

Would you agree with Suzy Menkes?

I'd say that a big part of what makes Daphne so appealing to the media is that she doesn't use fashion in order to promote her career in a different field. You know, she's not an actress who hires a stylist to look more interesting – the result being a bit too predictable most of the times. She is also not a professional member of the fashion industry who gets the clothes for free or who, like a lot of fashion editors, get money from their magazine to pay for their wardrobe. So in a way, whenever you see Daphne with her Cruella de Vil hair and her insane shoes and her outfits, it seems to come from a kind of disinterested, honest love of fashion – which makes her one of the only true fashion icons now.

She really doesn't accept gifts from designers?

Well, they want to give her clothes for free, for sure, but she insists on buying them because she believes in supporting avant-garde fashion. You know, the artistry that goes into couture, the collective historical knowledge of the specialists, the embroiderers, the feather makers, the so-called *petites mains*: all this could easily disappear if people didn't pay for those clothes anymore. And Daphne also has very personal and creative styling ideas herself: in our exhibition, for example, there was an outfit in which she put a short-sleeved Rick Owens coat back to front over a black sequinned coat that she had designed herself.

You could also look at the Daphne Guinness show in the context of the global boom of fashion exhibitions. Yves Saint Laurent at the Grand Palais in Paris, Alexander McQueen at the Metropolitan Museum in New York, plus thematic shows like *American High Style* or *30 Years of Japanese Fashion*. How do you assess this trend?

First of all fashion exhibitions are insanely popular with the public. In recent years they have broken records of visitor numbers in museums of all different sorts, be it art museums, history museums, design museums or specialized fashion museums. And they attract younger people, which seems a good way for museums to expand their audiences. You know, young people are the Holy Grail in museums.

But is the museum really the right place for fashion?

Well, the traditional complaint about fashion in museums is that it is static, that it looks like waxwork corpses behind glass, that the dresses don't move – somewhere along the lines of: fashion belongs on the streets. However, I have always thought that these complaints were overdrawn, not only because a lot of curators – including me – have been working very hard to try to animate the exhibits and not put them behind glass. Also, the museum strikes me as just another arena within which you can show fashion. We see fashion in real life, as you say, we see it on the internet, on television, in stores and shop windows. The museum provides a venue where you can look at it from perhaps a different, a more focused and detailed angle than when it's on the runway or in the shop.

What's irritating about fashion exhibitions is that they tend to present fashion as if it was art – while most fashion designers, when asked whether they see what they do as art, deny that.

That's true. I recently wrote an article for a collection of essays on fashion and art and I found that although there have been some designers who have argued that what they did was art – like Elsa Schiaparelli and Paul Poiret – the vast majority of them say: 'No, it's not art, it's part of daily life.' Also, a lot of people, many of them journalists, react badly to having fashion in museums because they think fashion is somehow this horrible corrupt commercial thing that is polluting the sacred ground of timeless high culture and the virginity of art. But I don't buy that. Art is also a gigantic multibillion-dollar business; it's as commercial as fashion. Nobody ever says that having a retrospective of an artist in a museum is immoral because it is going to increase his or her value. But they often say that about a retrospective of a fashion designer.

Rick Owens seems to take an altogether different stance: in his opinion, fashion has – in terms of self-referentiality and the usage of codes – by now surpassed art intellectually.

That's fascinating! I think that the idea that fashion is this superficial thing is totally wrong; it's a prejudice. And if someone like Rick Owens, who is really one of the few designers who advances fashion today in terms of creativity and style, recognizes that and addresses fashion's own intellectuality – I think that is fantastic!

The *Sparkle* section at the *Daphne Guinness* show; in front: catsuit and cape by Alexander McQueen

Helmut LANG

ARTIST

Long Island, New York

It was one of the most spectacular withdrawals in the history of fashion – followed by one of its most insistent rebirths. In October 2004, Helmut Lang, a master of intellectual minimalism, whose use of unexpected materials is expert, sold the last remaining shares in the brand he had founded in Vienna in 1977 and retreated to the seclusion of his Long Island farmhouse. Some time later, he reemerged as a visual artist. Lang, born in Austria in 1956, was no stranger to the world of art. While working as a designer, he was in close touch with Jenny Holzer and with Louise Bourgeois before her death in 2010. This interview took place in 2008 on the occasion of Lang's first solo exhibition at the kestnergesellschaft in Hanover, Germany.

Co-author: Philipp Ekardt

Mr. Lang, tell us how it came about that one of the style-defining fashion design-ers of the 1990s and early 2000s suddenly decided: That's it! Now I'm going to be an artist.

The idea didn't come out of the blue. I'd previously worked on art projects, but every activity requires total commitment. After spending 30 years working on clothes, it was simply time to make a decision – in favour of art, to put it bluntly. The change of frame-work gave me a new freedom, a freedom that I find very important.

In your first solo exhibition, *Alles gleich schwer*, on view in the kestnergesellschaft in Hanover, you show the disco ball and the three wooden eagles that previously were part of the interior of your boutique in SoHo in New York. There, they marked the entrance like landmarks. The disco ball is now heavily damaged, and

Helmut Lang, *Three* (2008), mahogany/tar, various sizes; photo: Elfie Semotan

the heads of the eagles have been sawn off. Looking at these objects, one can't help thinking: there really is no going back.

That's a justifiable interpretation for people who know these objects from their previous context. For me, however, they're raw materials in the best sense of the word. That is to say, I use these objects not as a reference, but because of their surface, their texture, their weight, and so on.

The famous graphic designer Peter Saville used the same combination, eagle and disco ball, in 2002 for his cover for the New Order compilation Retro *– as a reference to Helmut Lang?*

Peter Saville was indeed inspired by the objects in the boutique – in their original form. He also included a credit on the cover. But as I said, I'm not using the eagles and disco ball as a reference. As Louise Bourgeois once explained, when asked about the *subject* of art: 'Materials are just materials and they're there to serve you. The subject is never the materials, but what you want to express.' I believe her.

What do you want to express?

Three, the work with the eagles, is concerned with the realignment of values, with changes in the power structure and with emotional valences. *Next Ever After*, the mirror ball, is an interpretation of the Janus mythology, translated into our time. The background is that today we follow everything via the internet, but at the same time we are also observed via the internet, both in our private lives and in the public sphere. So it is now no longer a matter of simply looking forward and looking back in the tradition of the Janus mythology, but of a more multifaceted, voyeuristic behaviour, looking in many directions simultaneously – and the implications of this development.

Séance de travail, another of your works in the exhibition, also takes up the theme of seeing and being seen ...

The work dates from 1998, from a group exhibition I was in with Jenny Holzer and Louise Bourgeois at the Kunsthalle in Vienna. It's a video compilation

Helmut Lang, *Séance de travail, 1993–99* (1998), detail, video projection onto a mirror, 1,143 x 320 cm; photo: Elfie Semotan

of my fashion shows from 1993 to 1998, and it's projected onto a semi-transparent mirror wall. The projection and reflection collapse in a single plane; the viewers observe themselves in the mirror, becoming part of the work at the same time – without having been asked for permission. They become members of a society from which they're normally excluded.

In the spring of 1998, you decided to stream the presentation of a new Helmut Lang collection live via the internet. You were one of the first fashion designers to abandon the exclusivity of the fashion show in this way.

At the time, that was perceived as extremely radical. The work that's exhibited in Hanover dates from that same year. In those days I wanted to make the fashion show accessible to the general public. Today, it's quite normal for anyone to be able to follow exclusive fashion shows over the internet.

The way in which you divide up the exhibition space in Hanover with your *Séance de travail* installation recalls the proportions of your two former shops on Greene Street in New York: in your fashion boutique, but also in the perfume branch across the street, a very narrow side corridor was partitioned off from a spacious, gallery-like main room, as in the installation.

You could put it like that: I attempt to work with the space, and not against it.

You seem to be very interested in wood as a material: in Hanover, you're showing a number of wooden objects. Is that because you were previously unable to use wood? As a fashion designer, one seldom works with wood, unless one's a clog designer.

Actually, I've also designed clogs, clogs with a fur covering. But you're right, I do find it interesting today to work with materials that would not immediately make sense for a piece of clothing. Of course, it lies in the nature of the various disciplines that the materials are different – and I'm pursuing different aims.

Why did you choose the exhibition title *Alles gleich schwer,* 'All the same weight'?

The title expresses my belief in the equal status of human work. A famous work by Jenny Holzer is called *Everyone's work is equally important.* My exhibition is based on the idea that – in an age in which everything is changing, in which thoughts and feelings that are important for our existence are being questioned – everyone has to decide for themselves what weight they'll personally attach to the various areas of life. Cordula Reyer, a good friend of mine, has a recipe called just that: 'All the same weight.' The six eggs and the other ingredients all weigh the same, and then chance determines what will be on top. Viennese humour …

When you're just starting out as an artist – as you are – and you're friendly with important artists like Louise Bourgeois or Jenny Holzer, do you accept their advice? Do you show them your own work?

Jenny, Louise and I share a common past. We're used to working together, and we speak to each other regularly. My collaboration with Jenny dates back as far as 1996, when we were both represented at the Biennale in Florence in a joint exhibition. She showed one of her LED installations and I created an aroma installation in the same room. When Jenny creates something new, she mostly shows it to me, and it's much the same with

Louise, who recently got me involved in a magazine project, and who's also interested in my development. For me, this exchange feels perfectly normal; it's part of our relationship.

Is competition in the art world just as fierce as in the fashion world?

I can only answer this question with regard to the current situation. At the moment, I experience the art world as very cooperative and helpful. Perhaps that will change – who knows? But basically it's true to say that artists are generally used to working together. They often collaborate on projects and their works are shown together in group exhibitions. There's very little cooperation of this kind in the fashion world.

When you began designing fashion in Vienna in the 1970s, you were already deeply rooted in the art scene.

Yes, the person to whom I related most closely at that time was the artist Kurt Kocherscheidt, the first husband of the photographer Elfie Semotan, who was later married to Martin Kippenberger until his death. It's to Kurt Kocherscheidt that I owe my informal training and my understanding of art, so to speak. We spent a lot of time together, in Elfie's and Kurt's farmhouse in the countryside, where he also had one of his studios. There, I was able to witness his creative process. At that time, I was already working in fashion, but my approach was different compared with other designers – most of the things that inspired my work had very little to do with the classic fashion rituals. They were much more abstract. In that respect, I sometimes had the feeling that the fashion world was too restrictive for me.

As early as 2000, at the height of your success, you said in an interview with the German weekly Die Zeit: *'Society isn't changing as fast as the fashion world would like it to.' Did that comment already express a longing to slow down?*

Basically, the forced change in fashion always irritated me – I mean the idea that everything should be all new every six months. From the very beginning, I sympathized with the idea that fashion should consist of a combination of items with a long life and seasonal pieces. But what I really wanted to express then was the premonition I had that the fashion system, like all other systems, would need a radical realignment for the 21st century. I believed that globalization should not just result in higher quantitites, but that it would also have to go along with creative and ecological equality.

Nowadays you live and work in both New York and your farmhouse on Long Island. There's a rumour that you receive only one radio station, and that there's a beach nearby where Marilyn Monroe bathed in the nude during the 1950s.

The story about the radio is made up. We have satellite radio in the house, and I keep up to date with music anyway. My good friend Peter Kruder from Vienna sends me the best new releases regularly. But the story about Marilyn is supposedly true. The house in Amagansett in which she lived for a short time is just next door. Long Island has always attracted artists and famous personalities like Jackson Pollock, Willem de Kooning, Jackie Onassis, Lee Radziwill and many others. Andy Warhol's house is just ten minutes away, and the Rolling Stones worked in the vicinity, in Montauk.

Archive hl-art archive, Helmut Lang 1986–2005 (2008), video on five screens, installation at the 032c Museum Store, Berlin

Today, a very similar community of artists, celebrities and business profiteers still lives here.

Your first signs of life after leaving the fashion business were a number of editorial contributions that you published in various magazines. For example, excerpts from your *Selective Memory Series* were featured in the French magazine *Purple*. For this you used old correspondence, faxes, invitations and greeting cards from famous people like Martin Kippenberger, Nicole Kidman and Roman Polanski. You scanned them and made them illegible.

These were projects on which I worked 'in between' – they were partly archival and partly artistic. Some of them are basically endless, and I continue with them every day. The reason why I published extracts from them was that I wanted to gain time – time that I needed for myself, in order to be able to work on my art objects without being disturbed. I didn't want to start talking about what I was working on until I was actually finished. But since people kept asking me, 'So what are you doing at the moment?', these publications were my way of dealing with the interest without being distracted.

Parallel to the *Alles gleich schwer* exhibition in Hanover, you're also showing a digitalized archive of your fashion designs, aptly entitled *Archive*, in the 032c Museum Store in Berlin.

That's a purely archival project, documenting extracts from my collections between

ARCHIVE hl-art archive
Heimut Lang, 1986–2005

'Since I stopped taking an active part in the fashion scene, I haven't observed any dramatic changes in the silhouette.'

Archive hl-art archive, Helmut Lang 1986–2005 (2008), detail, video on five screens

1986 and 2005. The background here was that for many years I didn't have a clothing archive at all. I only began collecting my own pieces after I had moved to New York in 1997. For *Archive*, I had the individual pieces of the archive photographed digitally, because I'm not so interested in their physical presence. Now that the video exists, I'll probably sell off the physical archive in the near future.

When looking at the pieces of clothing rushing past on the five screens, one gets the impression of a certain proximity to art. Some of the designs show clearly how even in those days you had a very conceptual approach to questions of style: there is, for example, a creation that consists only of a zip fastener, a collar and a hip seam. Elements that are functional are shifted and transformed into a highly reduced intellectual ornament – or not?

You're referring to a piece from the series *Accessoire vêtements*, which was part of a textile language that I developed and which had central importance for my work. However, art is art and fashion is fashion – other conclusions are only permitted when they're made by other people.

Knowing that you initially started designing fashion in Vienna only because you couldn't find anything that you wanted to wear yourself, people probably wonder: what does Helmut Lang wear these days?

I still have enough of my own pieces so I manage very well. In any case, I've been wearing virtually the same things for a very long time. It may sound paradoxical, but as soon as you become a fashion designer, nobody expects you to look fashionable anymore. Unless you make it into an art form, like Karl Lagerfeld. But then you have to always put on a good performance – without exception.

You once said that the silhouette hasn't changed since the advent of techno. Do you find that you've missed out on a development since you stopped designing clothes?

It's only three and a half years since I stopped taking an active part in the fashion scene. Since then I haven't observed any dramatic changes in the silhouette. Perhaps something has become a bit narrower in one place and a bit wider elsewhere, but basically the definition is still the same. However, I do think that before long, fashion should react to the new realities.

Instead of, like pop music, getting involved in a succession of miniature retro trends?

That's what I call the unexpected downside of globalization. Of course it was exciting at first that everything went global, and that digital networks allowed for everything to grow together. But no one realized at the beginning that the global mainstream would become a threat to creativity. The music industry was the first to be hit by the effects. But also in other spheres it has become much more difficult to find an audience for a new, individual voice. Here, a countermovement will be needed.

You weren't present at the opening of your exhibition in Hanover, and you didn't attend the *Archive* presentation in Berlin personally either. That means you haven't had any direct feedback to your works. Don't you miss that?

I have to say I'm used to it. Even in the old days I never saw my presentations directly – I was always working backstage. And I never really liked the moment at the end of the show when the designer takes a bow on the catwalk. In that respect it suits me not to appear in person. I have learned to manage without the first spontaneous reactions. Reactions are important of course, but I don't need to have them immediately.

Is it true that you haven't been to Vienna since 1997?

Yes, it's true. Sometimes it seems like a very long time. Nowadays my idea of Austria is much nicer than it was when I lived there. I like this sentimental glorification from a distance – I find it not at all bad as a phenomenon; on the contrary, it's very helpful. There was a reason why I wanted to get away. Today, I think of Vienna with pleasure, but that doesn't mean that I want to return. Apart from that, most of my Austrian friends enjoy coming to visit me on Long Island.

Bruce WEBER

FASHION PHOTOGRAPHER

New York & Golden Beach, Florida

Without Bruce Weber, fine-rib, Y-fly white briefs wouldn't be what they are today: the epitome of male sexiness. Weber's black-and-white ad campaigns for Calvin Klein in the 1980s spawned both icons of advertising and ideals of natural, athletic (and very American) nudity. Born in Greensburg, Pennsylvania, in 1946, the photographer worked as a model himself for some time, appearing in photographs by Richard Avedon, among others. Today, Weber is also celebrated as a film-maker. His documentaries, most notably his tributes to jazz legend Chet Baker (*Let's Get Lost*, 1988) and to his beloved golden retriever (*A Letter to True*, 2003), exhibit the same intimate sensitivity as his photographs.

Mr. Weber, you're mostly known as a fashion photographer, but you make films, too. It's fascinating how they can neither be called documentaries nor fiction, but how they mix elements of both genres in a very personal, very dreamlike structure.

Definitely. My films all have this kind of classic old-school documentary style, but they also go crazy in parts, similar to the way I do my photography and my books. I want my films to be representative of my world, so I don't put a label on them asking: 'Is it a documentary or a feature, a short film or a film about poetry?' To me, they're just my films.

In Let's Get Lost, the acclaimed film on Chet Baker you made in 1988, and also in Broken Noses, your documentary on the American boxing champion Andy Minsker, which you finished one year earlier, you seem to almost stage reality – something you often do in your photography. For example in Broken Noses there is this one scene in which Andy Minsker is sitting in a restaurant and the waitress asks him for an autograph. It seems like you sent in the waitress only to make Minsker feel embarrassed and flattered ...

I didn't. I remember the waitress was really keen on meeting Andy. When we were filming in the restaurant, she came to me and asked: 'What's going on?' I explained to her we were shooting a film on Andy Minsker, the boxer. She knew who he was and she was very excited to meet him!

A similar scene is the one in Let's Get Lost: Chet Baker, the legendary jazz trumpet player, rides a bumper car at night surrounded by lots of beautiful young people partying and laughing ...

That scene we made up, you're right. But I don't know if I would call this staged reality. It's just my world, you know, and my world is a mixture of reality and fantasy. Sometimes fantasy becomes reality and vice versa.

You say in Broken Noses that Andy Minsker reminds you a lot of Chet Baker. Why is that?

It was because of his face. He had a little bit of Chet Baker's nose. But actually I guess the best way to explain this to you is to tell a story. Years ago, I really admired Clint Eastwood. I still do! When I was a kid, I used to watch *Rawhide* a lot, the TV show he did. I was so into that! Then when I started photographing people, men and women.

Peter Johnson, a wrestler discovered by Bruce Weber for modelling in 1996. Photo from the book *The Chop Suey Club* (Arena Editions, 1998

I wanted to make them all look like Clint Eastwood. Everybody in my pictures started to look like Clint Eastwood! Not that they'd all necessarily be wearing a cowboy hat, but, you know, girls, guys, young kids, everybody looked like Clint Eastwood! The girls would come up to me and say: 'Hey, I look a little masculine here!' The guys would say: 'Boy, I look pretty tough in this picture!' And parents would say to me: 'Mr. Weber, you've taken such a weird picture of my child!' It was in my mind and I couldn't get it out of there!

It's interesting how for some people similarities are obvious, while for others they are not. You also once said your father looked a lot like Paul Newman …

It's true, he did. I photographed Paul Newman once. It was when my dad was really ill. I had stopped working at the time, because of my dad, but I always had wanted to photograph Paul Newman, so that was the only job I accepted during the time my father was ill. I went out to the racetrack, where Paul was staying at the Holiday Inn. You know, he was a passionate racing driver, he even won several championships. I remember it turned out that he was in a really depressed mood that day, I don't know if he was worried about the race or what. So I finally said to him: 'Mr. Newman, I'm here to shoot a cover for a magazine on you. My dad's really ill. I just accepted the job because I wanted to see if you really look like my dad.' He looked at me like I was crazy. But it cheered him up a little. It's so sad Paul passed away.

Your film A Letter to True from 2003 is at the same time an antiwar statement and a love letter to your golden retriever, True. Why are you so fascinated with dogs?

I've had dogs since I was a kid growing up. They've always represented to me a close attachment to nature and a feeling of freedom. I've also learned a lot from my dogs – about body language, about the way they react to things, about their interest. They're intelligent but they almost have a childlike behaviour sometimes. I like that, because I feel that as a photographer you're also a child. Having a camera in your hand gives you a possibility of still being a kid.

You often use dogs in your fashion shoots. Is it true you first started doing this because you didn't like the clothes the models had to wear?

Well, first of all, I'm not the only photographer who uses animals in fashion shoots. It's been done for years and it was never a big deal. But it's true I sometimes put a lot of dogs in the shoots. Also lions, tigers, zebras and rhinos, because it helps the clothes …

It conceals them.

Well, if you have a dress that's not so pretty, it's best to put a rhino in front of it!

Has it ever happened that a model or yourself got attacked by an animal?

No, I must say that I've been very lucky. I'm knocking on wood! For example I've been with a surfer out by the ocean in California – Beau Young – he's the son of Nat Young, the famous Australian surfer. We were there with a lion. We had the animal trainer there, and as we were walking along the sea all of a sudden the lion turned around and stared angrily at Beau's board … Luckily the animal trainer was right there and distracted the lion with a piece of meat. I've also had a famous wrestler wrestling a bear for a shoot. The boy was really worried. We were all frightened! But I kind of got the pictures very

*'If you have
a dress that's
not so pretty,
it's best to
put a rhino
in front of it!'*

Bruce Weber's golden retriever, True, and the
elephant Thai. Still from the film *A Letter to
True* (2003)

quickly and then the bear jumped in the swimming pool – we couldn't get him out anymore! I was glad he did that instead of hurting the wrestler! I must say I'm very cautious now because I know I've been given a lot of chances.

<u>We are speaking about surfers, wrestlers, boxers. Can you explain your fascination with athletes?</u>

As I said earlier, I want my films and my photography to be representative of my own world. Athletes are part of my world. I know a lot of great athletes, like Muhammad Ali, and I know a lot of high school athletes, both men and women. What's interesting to me about them is their hunger to have something in their life, to *be* something, to win, the hunger to have a moment that shines – a golden moment. I like to be around when a person has that golden moment!

<u>In her famous collection of essays *On Photography*, published in 1977, Susan Sontag wrote: 'To take a photograph is to participate in another person's (or thing's) mortality, vulnerability, mutability' ...</u>

That's right. I guess I would say that a photograph has to have words. It doesn't necessarily have to have words written on it, and it doesn't have to change the world, but it has to say something to you, the photographer. It has to say something about what was going on in your life at that moment. Why did I take this picture of this person? Why did I meet this person?

Is it true you worked as a model yourself in the 1960s?

It's true, I did. I was doing it before I went to NYU film school. I needed some extra money because my parents didn't really want me to do what I was doing. They weren't supportive, you know. I knew a lot of photographers at the time. I was a skinny weird kid, so when they asked me to do pictures, it was fun.

You posed for Richard Avedon, right?

Yeah, for him and a lot of other great photographers. William Claxton, for example.

You interviewed William Claxton for *Let's Get Lost* because of the famous black-and-white photographs he took of Chet Baker in the 1950s …

Yeah, I adored these photographs! They were so beautiful.

Can the pictures you posed in as a model be seen anywhere?

Oh no, I'm really shy about them. I don't put them out in the world. I don't even have them hanging at my house.

But were they published in magazines at the time?

Oh yeah, all over the place! I mean I'm proud of these pictures, I learned a lot about photography by posing for them, and I also got to meet a lot of great photographers. But …

Did you pose nude?

No, I wish somebody had asked me! At the time I had a kind of okay body, so I guess I would have tried to do it. But probably it wouldn't have been such good pictures. I guess that's why nobody asked me.

What a shame. It would be nice to be able to look at them today …

That's what I always think when I'm doing nudes. I think that this person is going to be so glad to have these pictures in 30 or 40 years' time!

Has it become easier for you to get people to undress in front of your camera? One imagines that if Bruce Weber is shooting, the clothes must literally fly off the models …

Not really. I have the impression that

Chet Baker in Santa Monica, California (1987)

Ric Arango on a trampoline in
Backyard Movie (1990)

people are not so free anymore. It's more as if today, when you ask a person to be nude in a picture, you're asking them to call their grandmother first for permission. It's weird. Years ago you couldn't get the clothes back on people, today it's hard to get them off!

<u>Why is nudity still such an issue?</u>

I don't know! I think in general people are afraid to be nude because they don't understand how the vulnerability of it is very beautiful. Nudity seems so normal to me, but of course that's my world. I have my backyard where I take pictures of people running around nude all the time. I don't really think about it. One time, for example, I was making this movie in my backyard, a short film called *Backyard Movie*, and Ric Arango was flying up in the air nude …

The famous scene with the man and the dog jumping on the trampoline?

Yeah, that was in 1990. We never thought anything about it! But while we were shooting in my backyard, these two women came by walking on the beach and they almost fainted! Later, a policeman came up and asked: 'What's going on here?' I talked to him and explained that we were making a film and he said: 'Tell the guy not to jump so high.'

This scene also featured prominently in your video for the Pet Shop Boys hit 'Being Boring'. Why didn't you direct more music videos? You did three for the Pet Shop Boys and one for Chris Isaak. You must have had so many more offers from the music industry …

To be honest, I don't really enjoy doing music videos. I'm a great fan of music, I use a lot of music in my films. It's very close to me and my work. The reason I did Chris Isaak's video was that I was good friends with him, and I adore the Pet Shop Boys – Chris and Neal, they're so nice! But apart from that I never really wanted to do music videos because I felt that there were too many hands in the kitchen. If you're doing music videos, you have to get very involved with what the managers want, you have to deal with the record companies, all that. It feels like you have your hands tied.

Even if you don't have your hands tied there can be restrictions afterwards. When the Being Boring video came out it was banned by MTV in the US although it didn't show frontal nudity …

Exactly!

Poetry seems to be really important to you. In A Letter To True and in your film Chop Suey there are a lot of poems either being read out or you quote them in written form. Rilke, Whitman, Ginsberg …

I love poetry. I try to read a lot of it. I should start reading more. For example, I love Joseph Conrad – his books *Lord Jim* and *Youth* are so beautiful.

Do you know any poem by heart? Could you cite one now?

Any poem you mean? Sure, let's see … 'The way a crow / Shook down on me / The dust of snow / From a hemlock tree / Has given my heart / A change of mood / And saved some part / Of a day I had rued.' It's *Dust of Snow* by Robert Frost.

Beautiful! You also use a lot of poetic quotes from photographers in your films. In Chop Suey, for example, there's this one by Dorothea Lange reflecting on photography and on being a photographer. She says: 'One should really use the camera as though tomorrow you'd be stricken blind.'

That's so beautiful, and so true! You know, when you take a lot of pictures you just have to realize that it's a privilege to be able to take a picture. You have to say to yourself: 'Oh what a lucky man I am!' and accept the fact that you're lucky to have this experience. I've always felt that photography is not necessarily a matter of life and death. It is something of complete enjoyment but also something very fragile.

Who is the one person you haven't had the chance to photograph yet but whom you ultimately want to take a picture of?

My next puppy.

Picture credits

I wish to thank the following people for their kind help and support:

Joakim Andreasson • Karim Ben Geloun • Anne van den Bossche • Elisa Bürkle • Max Dax • David Flamée • Bruno Fulcrand-Rodriguez • Peter-Frank Heuseveldt • Heiko Hoffmann • Nathaniel Kilcer • Charlotte Knight • Mario Koell • Norman Konrad • Kiyoto Koseki • Jutta Kraus • Virginie Laguens • Soline Lamusse • Petra Lengnick • Eva Lindemann • Bianca Luzi • Karen Nitsche • Georgina Ordinas • Pablo Larios • Harald Peters • Kai von Rabenau • Jennefer Rossi • Romain Roz • Georg Rulffes • Timo Scherer • Florian Sievers • Ashley Smith • Claudia Stäuble • Divna Susa • Cornelius Tittel • Daniel Urrutia • Vanessa Vasquez • Anne Vegnaduzzo • Andreas Wesle • Wibke Wetzker

Thanks go as well to all of my interview partners – and especially to Philipp Ekardt.

Jan Kedves is a culture journalist and editor. He writes about pop, fashion and art. He was editor-in-chief of the German pop culture magazine *Spex* from 2010 to 2012, and his work has appeared in *frieze d/e*, *Süddeutsche Zeitung* and *Merkur*, among other publications. He lives in Berlin.

Front cover: Victoria Beckham, shot by Juergen Teller for Marc Jacobs, spring/summer 2008
Frontispiece: Look from Rick Owens' Lilies line, spring/summer 2013
Page 9: Runway look by Pierre Cardin, 1992

© Prestel Verlag, Munich • London • New York, 2013

© for the works reproduced is held by the artists, their heirs or assigns, with the exception of: Erwin Wurm with VG Bild-Kunst, Bonn 2013

Prestel Verlag, Munich
A member of Verlagsgruppe Random House GmbH

Prestel Verlag
Neumarkter Strasse 28
81673 Munich
Tel. +49 (0)89 4136-0
Fax +49 (0)89 4136-2335

www.prestel.de

Prestel Publishing Ltd.
14–17 Wells Street
London W1T 3PD
Tel: +44 (0)20 7323 5004
Fax + 44 (0)20 7323 0271

Prestel Publishing
900 Broadway, Suite 603
New York, NY 10003
Tel. +1 (212) 995-2720
Fax +1 (212) 995-2733

www.prestel.com

Library of Congress Control Number is available; British Library Cataloguing-in-Publication Data: a catalogue record for this book is available from the British Library; Deutsche Nationalbibliothek holds a record of this publication in the Deutsche Nationalbibliografie; detailed bibliographical data can be found under: http://dnb.d-nb.de

Prestel books are available worldwide. Please contact your nearest bookseller or one of the above addresses for information concerning your local distributor.

Project management by Claudia Stäuble
Assistance by Thorsten Schmidt
Copy-edited by Danko Szabo
Production by Friederike Schirge
Cover and design by Markus Weissenhorn
Typesetting by Greiner & Reichel, Cologne
Origination by Reproline Mediateam, Munich
Printed and bound by Neografia a.s.

Printed in Slovakia

Verlagsgruppe Random House FSC® N001967
The FSC® -certified paper Tauro was supplied by PapierUnion, Germany

ISBN 978-3-7913-4823-0